The Dynamic Terrorist Threat

An Assessment of Group Motivations and Capabilities in a Changing World

Kim Cragin • Sara A. Daly

Prepared for the

United States Air Force

Approved for Public Release; Distribution Unlimited

RAND

Project AIR FORCE

The research reported here was sponsored by the United States Air Force under Contract F49642-01-C-0003. Further information may be obtained from the Strategic Planning Division, Directorate of Plans, Hq USAF.

Library of Congress Cataloging-in-Publication Data

Cragin, Kim.
   The dynamic terrorist threat : an assessment of group motivations and capabilities in a changing world / R. Kim Cragin, Sara A. Daly.
      p. cm.
   "MR-1782."
   Includes bibliographical references.
   ISBN 0-8330-3494-4 (pbk. : alk. paper)
   1. Terrorism. 2. Terrorists. 3. Terrorism—United States—Prevention. 4.
Threats—United States—Prevention. 5. Behavioral assessment—United States.
I. Daly, Sara A. II. Rand Corporation. III.Title.

HV6431.C725 2003
303.6'25—dc22

                                                                          2003021106

The RAND Corporation is a nonprofit research organization providing objective analysis and effective solutions that address the challenges facing the public and private sectors around the world. RAND's publications do not necessarily reflect the opinions of its research clients and sponsors.

RAND® is a registered trademark.

Cover design by Stephen Bloodsworth

Published 2004 by the RAND Corporation
1700 Main Street, P.O. Box 2138, Santa Monica, CA 90407-2138
1200 South Hayes Street, Arlington, VA 22202-5050
201 North Craig Street, Suite 202, Pittsburgh, PA 15213-1516
RAND URL: http://www.rand.org/
To order RAND documents or to obtain additional information, contact
Distribution Services: Telephone: (310) 451-7002;
Fax: (310) 451-6915; Email: order@rand.org

Shortly after the September 11, 2001, terrorist attacks on the United States, Air Force Chief of Staff General John Jumper asked the RAND Corporation to conduct a study entitled "Thinking Strategically About Combating Terrorism." The yearlong project was divided into four research tasks, each undertaking different yet complementary aspects of the counterterrorism problem:

- **Threat assessment**—identifying the character and boundaries of the threat

- **The international dimension**—assessing the impact of coalition and other international actors on U.S. options

- **Strategy**—designing an overarching counterterrorism approach

- **Implications for the Air Force**—identifying promising applications of air and space power.

The research for this report was conducted as part of the first task on *threat assessment*. It assesses the threat that terrorist groups pose to the United States and to its interests overseas by proposing a framework for evaluating their relative motivations and capabilities. The report describes the tools that various terrorist groups use to maintain group cohesion and to conduct successful terrorist attacks. Also, after identifying the potential vulnerabilities of terrorist groups, it discusses how these groups adapt and change and concludes with implications for the ongoing struggle against terrorism. This report therefore should be of interest to policymakers confronted with the task of reducing the threat that terrorism poses to the United States today. But terrorist threats change over time, so the authors have attempted to present a framework of use to decisionmakers and academics involved in terrorism analyses and counterterrorism responsibilities in the future as well.

RAND publications stemming from the other three task elements listed above are the following:

David Ochmanek, *Military Operations Against Terrorist Groups Abroad: Implications for the U.S. Air Force*, MR-1738-AF.

Nora Bensahel, *The Counterterror Coalitions: Cooperation with Europe, NATO, and the European Union*, MR-1746-AF.

Olga Oliker, *The Counterterror Coalitions: Cooperation with the Post-Soviet States*, forthcoming.

C. Christine Fair, *The Counterterror Coalitions: Cooperation with Pakistan and India*, MG-141-AF.

This study was conducted as part of the Strategy and Doctrine Program of RAND Project AIR FORCE. Comments are welcome and may be addressed to the authors or to the acting program director, Alan Vick The authors completed the majority of the research for this report in 2002.

RAND PROJECT AIR FORCE

RAND Project AIR FORCE (PAF), a division of the RAND Corporation, is the U.S. Air Force's federally funded research and development center for studies and analyses. PAF provides the Air Force with independent analyses of policy alternatives affecting the development, employment, combat readiness, and support of current and future aerospace forces. Research is performed in four programs: Aerospace Force Development; Manpower, Personnel, and Training; Resource Management; and Strategy and Doctrine.

Additional information about PAF is available on our website at http://www.rand.org/paf.

CONTENTS

TABLES

Following the terrorist attacks of September 11, 2001, the U.S. government became engaged in a war on terrorism. Such a war has already required substantial military and diplomatic resources, and it is likely to require even more. Moreover, the war on terrorism will continue in the face of other competing U.S. strategic pursuits. It is essential, therefore, that the U.S. government prioritize its counterterrorism activities and conduct the war on terrorism as efficiently as possible.

The purpose of this report is twofold: first, it attempts to develop a matrix that helps policymakers identify the threat that terrorist groups pose to the United States; second, it assesses how terrorists adapt and change, to identify such groups' vulnerabilities. By combining these two approaches, the authors are able to suggest ways that the U.S. government can refine its counterterrorism policies. Thus, the report has direct relevance not only to the ongoing war on terrorism and those involved, but also to other audiences interested in the dynamic threat of terrorism.

UNDERSTANDING THE THREAT THAT TERRORISTS POSE TO THE UNITED STATES

To assess the various threats that terrorist groups pose to the United States, this report develops a threat framework, based on a step-by-step progressive analysis of terrorist groups' motivations and capabilities in the context of U.S. national security interests. The observation that militant organizations that employ terrorist tactics can be evaluated according to intent and capability is fairly logical. It is not revolutionary to view terrorists through the lens of *either* intentions *or* capabilities. Yet terrorism analysis rarely combines the two across the range of potential threats: that is, placing intentions on an x-axis and capabilities on a y-axis to measure terrorist groups against each other for threat salience. Indeed, terrorist threats are often gauged according to a specific group's members, skills, funds, and rhetoric. This approach makes it difficult to filter through the "noise" of the multiple threats facing the United States and isolate the most dangerous groups. (See pages 18–20.)

By combining an assessment of the intentions of various terrorist groups with their capabilities, the following matrix provides U.S. decisionmakers with a tool for prioritizing the threat of these groups.

Figure S.1 attempts to clarify the terrorist groups that pose the greatest threat to the United States. These groups demonstrate the highest degree of both capability and anti-U.S. intentions, as indicated by

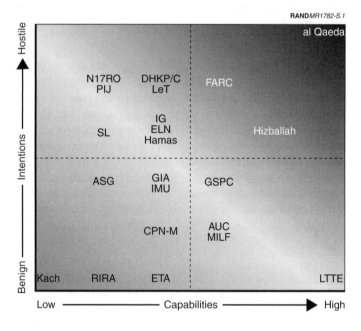

Figure S.1—Understanding the Relative Threats Posed by Terrorist Groups

the upper right-hand quadrant of the figure. According to the figure, three militant groups—al Qaeda, Lebanese Hizballah, and the Revolutionary Armed Forces of Colombia (FARC)—meet these criteria. As Chapter Two will explain in more detail, these three groups have demonstrated the highest degrees of both hostility toward the United States and capability to carry out sophisticated attacks. But the figure also highlights the degree to which other groups threaten the United States, as compared with each other. Thus, it illustrates that some highly capable groups, such as the Liberation Tigers of Tamil Eelam (LTTE), do not pose a significant threat to the United States because they have not demonstrated high degrees of anti-U.S. sentiment. In contrast, other groups, such as Jemaah Islamiya (not plotted in the figure), are not as capable but have demonstrated a willingness to attack U.S. citizens overseas. We stress the clarity that the matrix brings to our understanding of terrorist threats can help refine counterterrorism activities. (See pages 21–23.)

FACTORS THAT AFFECT TERRORIST GROUPS' CAPABILITIES

Next, we turn to a discussion on the tools that terrorist groups need to sustain and/or increase their *capabilities*. In the context of the above framework, these tools are the factors that affect a terrorist group's position and development along the x-axis. Thus, this section not only provides a deeper understanding of terrorists' requirements but also identifies potential points of vulnerability that would allow policymakers to reduce a particular group's overall capabilities.

To do this, we first divide terrorist groups' activities into two categories: activities that sustain the group's existence as a cohesive entity and activities that allow terrorists to conduct a series of successful attacks. We chose these two categories because the division clarifies the potential use of, and goals for, U.S. counterterrorism policy. For example, if U.S. policymakers want to prevent a particular attack or alleviate an immediate threat, then counterterrorism activities should focus, in general, on the second category. In comparison, if they want to completely dismantle a terrorist group over the long term, then counterterrorism activities should include a significant emphasis on the first category. (See pages 25–29.)

Second, we propose a list of tools that allow terrorists to sustain group cohesion, defining these tools as *organizational*. Alternatively, our second list of *operational* tools highlights the instruments used by terrorists to sustain a series of successful attacks.[1] Finally, we explore our understanding of these requirements and how they relate to terrorist groups' capabilities by using four groups as case studies: the Real Irish Republican Army (RIRA), the Palestinian group Hamas, FARC, and al Qaeda. We chose these groups because they represent different levels of operational capabilities, as indicated on the above matrix. As such, they illustrate a wide range of requirements for terrorist organizations. Table S.1 lists the organizational and operational tools. (See pages 29–59.)

THE DYNAMIC NATURE OF TERRORIST GROUPS

In our final chapter, we argue that the initial framework and the lists of terrorist requirements are still not quite enough. Policymakers can

Table S.1

Factors That Influence Terrorist Groups' Capabilities

Organizational Tools	Operational Tools
Ideology	Command and control
Leadership	Weapons
Recruitment pools	Operational space
Publicity	Training
	Intelligence
	Technical expertise and specialists
	External weapon sources
	Sanctuary
	Money
	Deception skills

---

[1]Although this categorization is different, it should be noted that RAND has researched the strategies, objectives, organizational structures, and capabilities of terrorist groups for over 30 years. Therefore, this framework and analysis of group capabilities should be viewed not as revolutionary, but rather as building on past research and methods for analyzing terrorism.

implement a counterterrorism policy that focuses on groups that threaten U.S. interests and design that policy to reduce terrorists' overall capabilities, but this alone might not be the most effective strategy, since terrorist groups can sometimes adapt quickly. Therefore, we explore the potential adaptations of terrorist groups. To do this, we examine the evolutionary trajectories of four terrorist groups: Shining Path (or Sendero Luminoso [SL]) in Peru, Hizballah, Egyptian Islamic Jihad (EIJ), and the Philippine Abu Sayyaf Group (ASG). We chose these groups because they exhibit different organizational structures, articulate different strategic objectives, and operate in different environments. Thus, similarities in their evolutionary trajectories are noteworthy. In particular, we focus on how the groups developed and strengthened, how they reacted to counterattacks and other state policies, and the factors that contributed to either their survival or their dissolution. We conclude that terrorist groups are the most vulnerable to counterterrorism activities when they go through periods of transition, especially if actions taken against them magnify the pressures forcing the evolution. (See pages 61–84.)

CONCLUSION

In sum, the purpose of this report is not to critique the U.S. security community or terrorism analysis in general. Rather, it is our belief that the very nature of terrorism makes it difficult to forecast new and emerging trends. Indeed, Bruce Hoffman highlights this difficulty in *Inside Terrorism*, stating, "The terrorist campaign is like a shark in the water: it must keep moving forward—no matter how slowly or incrementally—or die."[2] Thus, our purpose is to present a framework that allows policymakers to place parameters around the threat and yet still account for the dynamic nature of terrorist groups.

Notably, this tension between bounding the threat and maintaining the flexibility that terrorism analysis requires exists throughout the report. Yet the tension is by no means unique. RAND terrorism analysts have struggled with this challenge for more than 30 years—the

---

[2]Bruce Hoffman, *Inside Terrorism*, New York: Columbia University Press, 1998, p. 162.

1985 report titled *A Conceptual Framework for Analyzing Terrorist Groups* is an example of such an effort for dealing with the issue.[3] As such, this report should be read and understood as one of many tools that help policymakers develop and sustain an effective counter-terrorism strategy. (See pages 85–87.)

---

[3]Bonnie Cordes, Brian Michael Jenkins, Konrad Kellen, Gail V. Bass-Golod, Daniel A. Relles, William F. Sater, Mario L. Juncosa, William Fowler, and Geraldine Petty, *A Conceptual Framework for Analyzing Terrorist Groups*, Santa Monica, Calif.: RAND Corporation, R-3151, 1985.

ACKNOWLEDGMENTS

We would like to thank, first of all, our colleagues in the broader community of Project AIR FORCE's "Strategies for Countering Terrorism," of which this study was a part. In particular, we thank the project's leader, Edward Harshberger, Director of PAF's Strategy and Doctrine Program; Alan Vick, Associate Director of PAF; David Shlapak, task leader, who put a great deal of work into editing and revising the substance and prose of the text; Bruce Hoffman, RAND's Washington Office Director and Vice President of External Affairs, who provided much insight; and researchers Daniel Byman, Peter Chalk, Robert Mullins, John Parachini, and Matthew Wheeler, who contributed greatly in helping devise the methodology and build the framework. All the above-mentioned people assisted us in understanding various aspects of how terrorist groups operate and in comprehending the nature of the threat. We also greatly appreciate Dorothy Chen and Miriam Schafer's administrative help throughout the project.

We, of course, are responsible for any errors that remain.

ABBREVIATIONS

ASG	Abu Sayyaf Group
AUC	Self-Defense Forces of Colombia [Autodefensas Unidas de Colombia]
CBRN	chemical, biological, radiological, and nuclear
CPN-M	Communist Party of Nepal–Maoists
CPRS	Center for Palestinian Research and Studies
DHKP/C	Revolutionary People's Liberation Party/Front
DMZ	demilitarized zone
EIJ	Egyptian Islamic Jihad
ELN	National Liberation Army [Ejercito de Liberacion Nacional]
ETA	Basque Fatherland and Liberty [Euskadi Ta Askatasuna]
FARC	Revolutionary Armed Forces of Colombia
GIA	Armed Islamic Group
GSPC	Salafist Group for Preaching and Combat
Hamas	Islamic Resistance Movement
IG	Islamic Group [al-Gama'at al-Islamiyya]
IMU	Islamic Movement of Uzbekistan
LeT	Lashkar-e-Toiba

LTTE	Liberation Tigers of Tamil Eelam
MILF	Moro Islamic Liberation Front
MIPT	National Memorial Institute for the Prevention of Terrorism
MNLF	Moro National Liberation Front
NATO	North Atlantic Treaty Organization
N17RO	Revolutionary Organization November 17
PAF	Project AIR FORCE
PIJ	Palestinian Islamic Jihad
PIRA	Provisional Irish Republican Army
PKK	Kurdistan Workers' Party
PLO	Palestinian Liberation Organization
RIRA	Real Irish Republican Army
SDLP	Social and Democratic Labor Party
SL	Shining Path [Sendero Luminoso]
USS	United States Ship

Chapter One

INTRODUCTION

BACKGROUND

On September 5, 1972, eight Palestinians entered the dormitory of Israeli Olympians in Munich, West Germany, and kidnapped nine athletes.[1] By conducting this attack, the terrorists hoped to obtain the release of 236 Palestinian prisoners held by Israel, catapult their cause into the international spotlight, and make the presence of Palestinians felt at a gathering that had ignored them.[2] After hours of negotiations, the terrorists were allowed to move the hostages to a West German air base and planned to fly to Egypt for a prisoner exchange. But German police forces attempted to rescue the hostages, opening fire on the terrorists as the helicopters arrived. The rescue attempt failed spectacularly: All nine hostages were killed in subsequent firefights between the terrorists and police. Yet despite the loss of their hostages, the Palestinians and other terrorists learned two lessons: Terrorist attacks can be successful even if they fail to obtain their primary objective (which, in this case, was the release of Palestinian prisoners), and terrorist acts galvanize support, which, in turn, can strengthen terrorist organizations.[3] Indeed, to

---

[1]Bruce Hoffman, *Inside Terrorism*, New York: Columbia University Press, 1998, pp. 71–75.

[2]These comments by Abu Iyad, the Palestinian Liberation Organization's (PLO's) intelligence chief, are cited in Hoffman (1998, p. 73).

[3]In *Inside Terrorism*, Bruce Hoffman (1998, p. 74) states that following this attack, thousands of new Palestinians joined terrorist organizations, such as the Black September, that fought for the Palestinian cause.

many terrorism analysts, the events of September 1972 marked the advent of a period that Brian Jenkins described aptly in 1975 as "terrorism as theatre."[4]

Today, more than 30 years after Munich, the U.S. government finds itself engaged in a war on terrorism. This war is ambitious, targeting not only al Qaeda but also other affiliated groups scattered throughout the globe. Furthermore, it now appears that the basic terrorism aphorism—a lot of people watching and listening, but not a lot of people dead—has changed. As an example, al Qaeda has articulated that one of its primary objectives is to kill as many Americans as possible.[5] Thus, the U.S. policymaking community is determined to reduce the overall threat that terrorism poses to the United States. Indeed, statements from the White House have implied that the war on terrorism may eventually extend to other terrorists of *global reach*—that is, groups not connected to al Qaeda but those that have the capability to attack the U.S. homeland.[6] Such a war will likely require substantial military and diplomatic resources, lasting for at least several years. Moreover, the U.S. government will wage this war while pursuing other goals and protecting other interests on the international scene. This will surely create competition among national security objectives. It is essential, therefore, that the U.S. government prioritize its counterterrorism activities and conduct the war on terrorism as efficiently as possible.

METHODOLOGY

The purpose of this report is to help the U.S. government, particularly the Department of Defense and the intelligence community, identify the most immediate, as well as emerging, terrorist threats and to provide some insights into how best to defeat them. Historically, U.S. intelligence and security communities have taken an

---

[4]Brian Jenkins, cited in Hoffman (1998, p. 38).

[5]For a discussion of al Qaeda and its objectives, see Peter Bergen, *Holy War, Inc.: Inside the Secret World of Osama Bin Laden*, New York: The Free Press, 2001, pp. 24–40.

[6]The term "global reach" is taken from a December 2001 speech by President Bush in which he stated, "American power will be used against all terrorists of global reach" (www.whitehouse.gov/news/releases/2001/12/20011220-11.html, accessed September 2003).

"intuitive" approach to evaluating the relative threat posed by terrorist groups. To do this, analysts have ranked terrorists from most to least threatening based on the number of attacks they have carried out against U.S. and other Western targets within a specific time frame. Alternatively, analysts have assessed the strengths and weaknesses of a specific group according to its modus operandi, number of fighters, and degree of support, but have not systematically compared it with the threat posed by other terrorist organizations. Although ranking groups in this way appears the most logical in the short run, it does not provide the policymaker with a sense of how terrorist group capabilities change over time. Similarly, such an approach does not take into account, for example, the threat posed by groups that have not recently carried out an attack against U.S. targets but rather have spent time deepening the anti-U.S. sentiment of its members and supporters. We argue that these seemingly inactive groups might pose a more significant threat to the United States in the medium-to-long term.

This report intends to reveal the dynamic between capabilities and intentions of terrorist groups as well as what this means to the United States. Furthermore, we attempt to develop a systematic approach that policymakers can use to assess terrorist threats over time. Finally, we hope that the report will provide insight for policymakers as they determine if and when the U.S. government should intervene in the development of a terrorist group in order to interrupt its expansion.

To do this, we first assess existing terrorist threats to the United States, utilizing an analytical framework that allows us to compare the motivations and capabilities of terrorist groups *against each other*. We developed this framework, outlined further in Chapter Two, by starting with an examination of historical patterns of terrorist activities.[7] For example, from 1991 to 2000, the RAND Terrorism

---

[7]The numbers presented in this report are drawn from the RAND Terrorism Chronology and the RAND-MIPT [National Memorial Institute for the Prevention of Terrorism] Terrorism Incident Database, unless otherwise noted. A version of this Chronology and Database are available online at http://db.mipt.org. We note, however, the danger in relying too much on past trends of terrorist attacks to predict the future. Indeed, one of our primary stipulations throughout this report is that terrorist groups are dynamic entities. As such, the data presented in this report simply provide a wider context for our analyses. For more information, see the Appendix.

Chronology and RAND-MIPT Terrorism Incident Database recorded approximately 3,800 international terrorist attacks. We used this database to examine the modus operandi and capabilities of various terrorist groups (this information can be found in the Appendix). However, relying on historical data presents a problem to the counterterrorism analyst: Not all terrorist groups that have been active since 1991 pose a threat to the United States, nor do many of the weapons and tactics used by these groups pose a particular challenge. In addition, historical trends cannot necessarily be used to accurately predict future terrorist attacks. To address this difficulty, we overlay the historical patterns discovered with our evaluation of emerging terrorist trends.

Chapter Two then rates 22 terrorist organizations on two dimensions: their overall capabilities for violence and the degree of their hostility toward the United States. Rating these groups by no means provides a complete picture of terrorism to the reader; rather, we chose groups that represent a range of both capabilities and intentions vis-à-vis the United States. We then highlight three groups that, according to the framework, present the greatest threat to the United States and its interests.

Having established a framework for comparing the threats that various terrorist groups pose to the United States, we provide in Chapter Three a more comprehensive analysis of terrorists' capabilities. Chapter Three examines what terrorist groups need to sustain or increase their capabilities and, by doing so, also identifies potential targets for U.S. counterterrorism activities. To do this, we divide the groups' needs into organizational and operational tools: what terrorist groups need to *exist* and what they need to effectively *conduct attacks*.

The division of existing and conducting attacks has a significant impact on U.S. counterterrorism policy objectives. For example, any government's use of media campaigns designed to reduce public support for terrorism and therefore future recruits actually targets terrorists' organizational requirements or their existence. Such policies may have an impact on terrorist groups' abilities to conduct attacks, but only because they threaten the very existence of the organization itself. In contrast, policies that attempt to limit terrorists' access to chemical, biological, radiological, or nuclear (CBRN) materials are targeting terrorist groups' operational capabilities, not their actual existence. Either policy can be effective, but each has different results. After dividing terrorist groups' needs into organizational and operational requirements, we use observations drawn from four groups—Northern Ireland's Real Irish Republican Army (RIRA), the Palestinian group Hamas, the Revolutionary Armed Forces of Colombia (FARC), and al Qaeda—to illustrate how these requirements might change as groups attempt to increase the sophistication and impact of their attacks.

Chapter Four adds a final dimension to our analysis by examining how terrorists react to dynamics within their own organizations as well as in their surrounding environments. The chapter provides insight into potential shifts in the current terrorist threat environment. To do this, we use four additional case studies—the Philippine Abu Sayyaf Group (ASG), Peru's Shining Path (or Sendero Luminoso [SL]), Lebanese Hizballah, and the Egyptian Islamic Jihad (EIJ)—to demonstrate how the motivations, objectives, tactics, and targets of terrorist groups might change. Indeed, the primary conclusion we draw from Chapter Four is that, as terrorist groups go through periods of transition, they exhibit unique vulnerabilities, which can then be exploited by U.S. counterterrorism activities.

Chapter Two

ASSESSING TERRORIST THREATS

This chapter develops a framework for evaluating the threats that various terrorist groups pose to the United States, using the twin criteria of *intentions* and *capabilities*.[1] To do this, we first establish five degrees of anti-U.S. sentiment, our measure of particular terrorist groups' desire to attack the U.S. homeland and U.S. interests overseas. Similarly, we also articulate five different capability indicators for militant organizations that conduct terrorist attacks. By understanding terrorist groups in this framework, policymakers can compare the relative threats that such groups pose to the United States. Finally, we apply this framework, evaluating 22 terrorist groups according to their hostility toward the United States and their overall capabilities.

BUILDING THE FRAMEWORK

Our analytical framework has three logical components. The first component is its overall structure, which ranks metrics of *intent* and *capability* against each other. Although terrorism analysts have not historically used such a systematic approach to evaluate threats, this is, in fact, the traditional manner of evaluating threat in strategic studies and defense planning. Thus, the first component simply represents an adaptation of more-traditional defense analyses to the world of terrorism studies.

---

[1]Note that this report does not assess the threats posed by terrorists not associated with an organized group, such as Oklahoma City's bomber Timothy McVeigh.

The second component of the framework is the actual *metrics* themselves: *anti-U.S. sentiment* for intent and *demonstrated and perceived attack skills* for terrorist capability.[2] Of course, terrorist groups represent a wide range of potential motivations, decisionmaking, modus operandi, and operational environments; this variety has always been the most contentious element in comparing the threats that terrorist groups pose to the United States *against each other*. We chose these particular metrics because we believe that they are specific enough to provide measurable criteria and yet still allow us to capture the variety of different militant organizations that engage in terrorist activities. Notably, we designed these metrics to highlight terrorist threats to the United States, not international terrorism in general. We acknowledge that there may be other ways of measuring intent and capability: The value of the framework is not as much tied to the metrics used as to the fact that there *are* identifiable metrics.

Finally, the third component is a set of ten *thresholds* we established within the two metrics to indicate multiple degrees of intent and capability. We based the thresholds on trends in terrorist activities over the past 30 years, overlaying this historical analysis with our assessment of more-recent and emerging patterns (see the Appendix for more details). Like the previous component, the purpose of these thresholds is to create a structured analytical model while still being flexible enough to account for the diversity among terrorist groups. Once again, we do not expect the reader to necessarily accept our specific thresholds: Their true value lies in the fact that they are clearly defined and exist along a measurable continuum.

The following sections further outline and apply these thresholds to the current and emerging terrorist threat environment.

---

[2]As mentioned in the introduction to this analysis, we used numbers drawn from the RAND Terrorism Chronology and RAND-MIPT Terrorism Incident Database to arrive at these metrics. But the authors also add a level of *perceived skill* in addition to demonstrated skill. When applicable, this subjectivity is highlighted and explained in the text. We do not believe that it detracts from the utility of the framework, however, and think that other metrics could also be used successfully.

Indicators of Terrorists' Intentions

We chose "anti-U.S. sentiment" to measure the intentions of terrorist groups vis-à-vis the United States. Of course, some groups do not articulate or demonstrate *any* anti-U.S. sentiment. For example, Kach is a right-wing Israeli terrorist group accused of conducting terrorist attacks on Palestinians in Israel and has not articulated grievances against the United States or U.S. strategic interests[3] overseas. For the purposes of this report, therefore, the first threshold within the metric *anti-U.S. sentiment* is the next level above *nothing*. Accordingly, the following section describes five anti-U.S. sentiment thresholds that build on each other and are listed in ascending order.

The first threshold is *anti-U.S. rhetoric and/or a stated goal of destabilizing important U.S. partners*. By itself, this threshold indicates relatively low degrees of anti-U.S. sentiment. Indeed, many terrorist groups espouse hatred for the United States and yet do not attack U.S. citizens, businesses, or interests overseas. For example, the Nepalese Maoists form a left-wing militant organization that uses anti-U.S. "imperialist" and "capitalist" rhetoric, but they only attack local Nepalese targets.[4] Thus, terrorists within this threshold (like the Maoists) have not followed their anti-U.S. rhetoric with attacks on U.S. targets, which logically places them lower on an "anti-U.S. sentiment" continuum than the groups that *do* attack U.S. targets.

The next threshold is an *association with another terrorist group that specifically seeks to target U.S. citizens and institutions*. We established this as a distinct threshold, which is primarily based on the model of training and support that al Qaeda has provided to other, more regionally focused, terrorist groups in recent years. Although

---

[3]It is arguable that terrorist attacks that disrupt the Middle East peace process are against U.S. interests. However, we are mostly examining strategic interests, or those that have direct implications for U.S. national security strategy and the war on terrorism.

[4]The CPN-M is a group that controls sections of Nepal, including Rukum, Rolpa, Salyan, Kalikot, and Jagarkot, and has extended its influence into other areas, such as Sindhuli, Solukhumba, Khotang, Sankhuwasabha, and Okhaldhunga. The group conducts insurgency campaigns in rural Nepal as well as terrorist attacks in urban centers. Peace talks between the Maoists and the Nepalese government deteriorated in July 2001. For more information, see R. Bedi, "'Red Terror' Gaining Ground in Nepal," *Jane's Terrorism and Security Monitor*, July 2, 2002.

such terrorist organizations as the PLO, Spain's Basque Fatherland and Liberty (ETA), and the Provisional Irish Republican Army (PIRA) have historically maintained informal relationships, this pattern of training and sponsoring other terrorist groups is relatively new and at this point unique to al Qaeda. Despite al Qaeda's support, however, many of its affiliates do not attack U.S. targets. Instead, they provide logistical support or sanctuary to al Qaeda members. As such, this association appears to represent a higher degree of anti-U.S. sentiment than simple rhetoric but not as much as if the affiliated group specifically targeted the United States. For example, although the Salafist Group for Preaching and Combat (GSPC) is an Algerian Islamist group affiliated with al Qaeda, it has not attacked U.S. targets.[5] It is therefore logical that the GSPC poses a greater threat to the United States, solely in regards to intentions, than the Nepalese Maoists do. However, the GSPC is still not as threatening as a terrorist organization that specifically targets U.S. citizens or businesses.

Similarly, the third threshold is an *explicitly anti-Western ideology and/or a history of significant attacks on important U.S. partners.* Some terrorist groups, such as the Pakistani terrorist group Lashkar-e-Toiba (LeT), do not attack U.S. targets but *do* present a clear and immediate danger to important U.S. partners. Notably, just as U.S. national security interests adjust over time, so also may the terrorist groups that fall above this threshold. In the context of the war on terrorism, Pakistan is a strategic ally. Therefore, terrorist groups that have a history of significant attacks on Pakistan would rate higher on our *intent* metric than a group like the Algerian GSPC or the Nepalese Maoists.

The fourth threshold consists of groups that *target U.S. citizens and/or property in pursuit of their local agenda.*[6] Some terrorist

---

[5]The GSPC never formally signed the *fatwa* issued by the World Islamic Front for Jihad Against the Jews and Crusaders, opting instead to associate with al Qaeda under its own terms. See Rohan Gunaratna, *Inside Al Qaeda: Global Network of Terror,* New York: Columbia University Press, 2002, p. 125.

[6]This threshold might include a group that kills foreigners to put pressure on the targeted state or local authorities. This threshold is in contrast to attacks conducted in areas where the victims may or may not be foreigners (e.g., a shopping mall). Or, similarly in contrast, some groups specifically tell their members not to kill or target foreigners.

groups specifically attack U.S. targets but do so to promote a local agenda. FARC, for example, has launched multiple attacks on U.S.-owned oil pipelines as part of its campaign to destabilize the Colombian government.[7] These attacks are not necessarily aimed at the United States, yet they still demonstrate a higher degree of anti-U.S. sentiment than simple rhetoric or attacks on important partners.

Finally, the highest threshold incorporates terrorist groups that *specifically focus their attacks on U.S. targets.* The most prominent terrorist group within this threshold is, of course, al Qaeda, which has attacked U.S. embassies, warships, and perpetrated the attacks of September 11, 2001. In addition, other terrorist acts, such as the 1983 U.S. Marine barracks bombing or the Pan Am 103 hijacking, have specifically targeted the United States as part of a wider international agenda.

Having established five thresholds of anti-U.S. sentiment that can be used to measure the intentions of terrorist groups, it is useful to illustrate how these thresholds might be used to assess terrorist threats. To do this, we assign each threshold a numerical value (see Table 2.1) and then use these values to compare terrorist groups' intentions toward the United States against each other.

Table 2.1

Indicators of Terrorist Groups' Intentions

Thresholds of Anti-U.S. Sentiment	Numerical Value
Anti-U.S. rhetoric and/or a stated goal of destabilizing important U.S. partners	1
Association with another terrorist group that seeks to target U.S. citizens and institutions	2
Explicitly anti-Western ideology and/or a history of significant attacks on important U.S. partner	3
Targeting U.S. citizens and/or property to pursue a local agenda	4
Specifically focusing attacks on U.S. targets	5

[7]For more information on FARC's articulated objectives, see "La Paz Sobre la Mesa," *Cambio*, May 11, 1998, pp. 14–21.

In conclusion, the purpose of this intent metric is to provide a list of relatively objective criteria with which to measure terrorist groups' desire to attack the United States and U.S. interests overseas. As such, it is only half of the picture. But it does allow analysts to compare the threats posed to the United States by equally capable groups: For example, the Liberation Tigers of Tamil Eelam (LTTE) is a highly capable group, similar to FARC, but it has not demonstrated any anti-U.S. sentiment; therefore, according to Figure 2.1, the LTTE would be assigned the numerical value "0," while FARC would be categorized as a "4." The utility of this metric, therefore, is that it allows policymakers to identify group distinctions and focus U.S. counterterrorism policy accordingly.

Similarly, the framework can also help distinguish between terrorist groups with similar ideologies but different intentions. For example, both al Qaeda and Hamas are Islamist groups, but the former is waging what could be interpreted as a war against the United States, while the latter confines its attacks almost exclusively to targets within Israel and the Occupied Territories. As a result of their similar ideologies, these groups are often conflated into one threat category: Islamist terrorists. However, from a U.S. perspective, al Qaeda's intentions are much more of a threat than are those articulated by Hamas.

Indicators of Terrorist Capabilities

While it is useful to examine terrorist groups according to intent, it is also important to assess the organizations' ability to actually carry out attacks on their intended adversaries. To do this, we chose five "capability indicators," basing them on our analysis of international terrorist attacks drawn from the RAND Terrorism Chronology and RAND-MIPT Terrorism Incident Database. As mentioned above, the RAND databases have recorded approximately 3,800 international terrorist attacks from 1991 through 2000. Yet not all of these attacks threatened the United States or U.S. citizens overseas. Figure 2.1 illustrates this point, comparing the overall patterns in international terrorist attacks with attacks directed against U.S. targets.

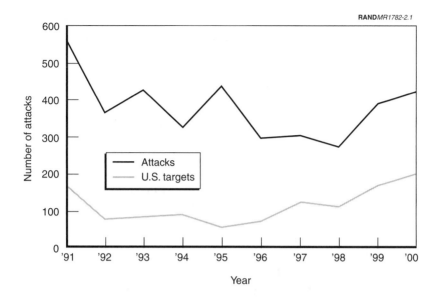

Figure 2.1—International Attacks as Compared with Attacks Directed Against U.S. Citizens and Property Overseas

It is clear from Figure 2.1 that the number of terrorist attacks on U.S. targets overseas has increased steadily since 1995.[8] This figure also raises the questions "What terrorist groups are responsible for this increase?" and "Which groups will pose the greatest threat to U.S. national security interests in the future?" In answering these questions, it is important to note that the historical data are illustrative only of trends in terrorist attacks and are not predictive. We therefore add our own assessment of new and emerging terrorist trends. The result is a series of criteria that, we believe, provide enough structure to form a framework for measuring terrorists' capabilities yet are flexible enough to account for the multiple operating environments and state counterterrorism capabilities encountered by militant

---

[8]The numbers in this figure are taken from the RAND-MIPT Terrorism Incident Database and the RAND Terrorism Chronology. Note that RAND discontinued its Chronology in 1998 and did not restart the project until April 2001. RAND has begun to fill in this "gap" and has, at this point, supplemented its Chronology with information from the U.S. Department of State's *Patterns of Global Terrorism*, which uses a definition of terrorism that is closely related to the RAND data.

organizations that conduct terrorist attacks. Notably, these indicators are not meant to be either exclusive or comprehensive, in the sense of identifying all relevant or potential types of attacks that a group might contemplate. Instead, the indicators provide policymakers with a series of measures that they can use to compare terrorists' relative capabilities.

Like the previous section, the following capability thresholds begin one level above simply conducting an attack. For example, on March 12, 2002, two al-Fatah members threw grenades in the direction of Israeli vehicles traveling near the Lebanese border in Israel, killing six people and wounding seven. Attacks at this level do not necessarily require reconnaissance, technical expertise, or even prior planning. Indeed, the attack described above simply required the terrorists to obtain grenades and plan minimal degrees of operational security to get to the attack site without being caught, both of which are relatively easy in Israel and the Occupied Territories. As such, the attack does not provide much insight into al-Fatah's operational capabilities as an organization.

It is noteworthy, however, that most of the terrorist attacks worldwide occur at this level. For example, from January 1998 through December 2002, terrorists averaged approximately one death and three injuries per attack.[9] Because we begin our first threshold one level above *anything*, as described below, illustrates the fact that many terrorist groups may not even meet the requirements for the first threshold. Moreover, just because a group *does* meet this requirement does not mean that the organization's *every attack* occurs over the first threshold. To gauge threats against the United States, we set our first threshold high in the spectrum of overall trends of terrorist attacks. The five thresholds are described below in ascending order. (For more information on the historical patterns of terrorist attacks as they relate to these thresholds, see the Appendix.)

The first capability threshold is the ability to *kill or injure on the order of 50 people in a single attack*. We chose this threshold as an indicator of a terrorist group's ability to acquire basic knowledge of a

---

[9]This estimate includes possible suicide bombers who die as a result of an attack, although the number of these types of attacks is not very significant; suicide attacks account for approximately 1/10 of all attacks, if that many.

target, maintain some low degree of technical competence (e.g., the capacity to build an improvised explosive device), and to plan and execute an attack with similarly minimal levels of operational security. For example, in January 1998, the Armed Islamic Group (GIA) threw an improvised explosive device into a movie theater in Algeria, killing approximately 50 people. Although it was not a particularly sophisticated attack, the outcome indicates that the group has sufficient planning and execution skills to successfully target a concentrated group of people.

We established the next terrorist capability threshold as the ability to *intentionally target unguarded foreign nationals.* Our analysis of the data suggests that *deliberate* attacks on foreigners require a higher degree of reconnaissance, technical expertise, and planning than does the previous threshold. Furthermore, while some terrorist groups might be able to kidnap or assassinate foreigners once or twice during their existence, this level of operation is difficult for many terrorist groups to sustain. An example of this type of act is the May 8, 2002, attack by Pakistani terrorists against French engineers residing in Karachi's Sheraton Hotel, which killed 13 and injured 25. In this attack, the perpetrators apparently knew not only the location of the victims but also their travel schedule to and from work. Therefore, in our judgment, this threshold represents a higher degree of capability than does killing 50 individuals.

The third threshold for measuring terrorist groups' capabilities is the ability to *kill or injure 150 or more people in an attack*—an example of this is the December 21, 1988, bombing of Pan Am flight 103 over Lockerbie, Scotland, which killed 270 people in the air and on the ground.[10] For this threshold, we decided to move beyond historical patterns of terrorist attacks and also account for emerging trends in terrorist activities. This threshold justifies such a shift because, at this level, it is difficult to separate the *intent* to kill 150 or more people from the actual *ability* to do so. For example, EIJ has not killed more than 150 in a single attack, even during the peak of its campaign in Egypt in the early 1990s. Therefore, if we were to simply abide by past patterns of EIJ attacks, this absence could be interpreted as a lack of

---

[10]For more information on the Pan Am attack, visit the memorial website at www. geocities.com/CapitolHill/5260/headpage.html (accessed September 2003).

ability to conduct such an attack and the EIJ would not fall above this third threshold. Yet EIJ members did play a significant role in the planning and execution of the U.S. embassy bombings in Nairobi and Kenya, which killed more than 150 people.[11] So, clearly the EIJ's role in these attacks appears to indicate its ability to kill 150 or more people, even though the group had not done so in the past. Therefore, this threshold attempts to capture both the demonstrated and *perceived* ability of terrorist groups.

Similarly, we established the fourth threshold as the demonstrated and perceived ability of terrorist groups to *strike at guarded targets*. In this context, an attack on a guarded target includes successful penetrations of U.S. military facilities or embassies, in contrast with standoff attacks, such as drive-by shootings. For example, on July 24, 2001, the LTTE attacked a combined Sri Lankan Air Force base and civilian airport, destroying eight military and six civilian aircraft.[12] In many ways, the repertoire of skills needed to conduct an attack against guarded targets, like the Sri Lanka example, is suited more to guerrilla organizations than to terrorists.[13] Guerrilla groups tend to focus their attacks on military targets, using assault rifles and bombs to gain control over people and territory. In contrast, terrorist groups use violence to draw attention to their political objectives or to pressure governments into changing their policies.[14] Thus, guerrilla groups with insurgent agendas, such as the LTTE or FARC, work to develop the skills and weapons needed to successfully attack police and military or guarded targets. Having said that, some terrorist groups do successfully attack guarded targets, as demonstrated by the aggression against U.S. embassies overseas. Therefore, the skills required for terrorist groups to conduct an attack on guarded targets merit their own threshold.

The highest terrorist capability indicator that we incorporated into this framework is the *ability to coordinate multiple attacks*. We chose this threshold because such attacks require sophisticated planning,

---

[11]Gunaratna (2002, pp. 97, 159–164).

[12]John Daly, "Will Sri Lanka's Peace Accord with the Tamil Tigers Hold?" *Jane's Terrorism and Security Monitor*, April 1, 2002.

[13]Note that this framework does *not* examine insurgency capability indicators.

[14]Hoffman (1998, pp. 41–44).

intelligence gathering, operational security, technical expertise, and command and control. Indeed, for the purpose of this analysis, multiple "coordinated" attacks do not include relatively minor degrees of coordination, such as the November 2002 attacks on a Nairobi hotel and Israeli jetliner. This attack did not require a high level of technical expertise (simply crashing into a hotel or firing a portable air defense system), operational security, planning, or even a significant level of coordination. In contrast, the September 11, 2001, attacks on the United States *are* representative of this threshold. For example, it now appears that, in 1997, al Qaeda operatives conducted reconnaissance missions throughout the United States, filming such potential targets as the Statue of Liberty and Disneyland,[15] and some of the hijackers, such as Mohammad Atta, enrolled in flight schools in preparation for the attack.[16] Although al Qaeda is currently the pre-eminent anti-U.S. group that coordinates multiple sophisticated attacks, other groups (such as the LTTE) have also demonstrated this ability. One can therefore imagine that other groups might attempt to conduct a series of coordinated attacks inside the United States or against U.S. targets overseas.

As with the indicators of terrorist groups' intentions, we next assign each of these thresholds a numerical value. Table 2.2 identifies these values, which we then use in the next section to demonstrate how terrorist groups' capabilities can be compared against each other.

Table 2.2

Indicators of Terrorist Groups' Capabilities

Thresholds of Demonstrated and Perceived Attack Skills	Numerical Value
Kill or injure 50 or more people in a single attack	1
Intentionally target unguarded foreign nationals	2
Kill or injure 150 or more people in a single attack	3
Strike at guarded targets	4
Successfully coordinate multiple attacks	5

---

[15]"Al-Qaeda Suspect Filmed WTC," *CNN.com*, July 16, 2002.

[16]For more information, see Bergen (2001, pp. 35–36).

APPLYING THE FRAMEWORK

Having established a framework that can be used to compare terrorist threats posed to the United States by a variety of different militant groups, this section categorizes 22 terrorist groups into the two-dimensional space that we have defined. Table 2.3 lists these groups

Table 2.3

Applying the Framework to 22 Terrorist Groups

Group	Acronym or Short Name	Home Base
al Qaeda	al Qaeda	Afghanistan
Abu Sayyaf Group	ASG	Philippines
Self-Defense Forces of Colombia [Autodefensas Unidas de Colombia]	AUC	Colombia
Communist Party of Nepal–Maoist	CPN-M	Nepal
Revolutionary People's Liberation Party/Front	DHKP/C	Greece
National Liberation Army [Ejercito de Liberacion Nacional]	ELN	Colombia
Basque Fatherland and Liberty [Euskadi Ta Askatasuna]	ETA	Spain
Revolutionary Armed Forces of Colombia	FARC	Colombia
Armed Islamic Group	GIA	Algeria
Salafist Group for Preaching and Combat	GSPC	France
Islamic Resistance Movement	Hamas	West Bank and Gaza
Party of God	Hizballah	Lebanon
Al-Gama'at al-Islamiyya	IG	Egypt
Islamic Movement of Uzbekistan	IMU	Uzbekistan
Kach	Kach	Israel
Lashkar-e-Toiba	LeT	Kashmir
Liberation Tigers of Tamil Eelam	LTTE	Sri Lanka
Moro Islamic Liberation Front	MILF	Philippines
Revolutionary Organization November 17	N17RO	Greece
Palestinian Islamic Jihad	PIJ	West Bank and Gaza
Real Irish Republican Army	RIRA	Northern Ireland
Shining Path [Sendero Luminoso]	SL	Peru

alphabetically according to the acronym or short name by which they are most commonly known. Notably, analysts could easily include any number of terrorist groups in this framework; we have chosen the following 22 groups because they represent a wide variety of motivations, capabilities, and relevance to the war on terrorism.

We next coded each group according to the set of five thresholds for anti-U.S. sentiment and the five levels of capability indicators, as described above. The results of this coding are listed in Table 2.4 and displayed graphically in Figure 2.2. Intentions are ranked from 0 to 5 based on the ascending order of anti–U.S. sentiment indicators, with

Table 2.4

Coding Terrorist Groups for Intentions and Capabilities

Group	Intentions	Capabilities
al Qaeda	5	5
ASG	2	1
AUC	1	3
CPN-M	1	2
DHKP/C	4	2
ELN	3	2
ETA	0	2
FARC	4	3
GIA	2	2
GSPC	2	3
Hamas	3	2
Hizballah	3	4
IG	3	2
IMU	2	2
Kach	0	0
LeT	4	2
LTTE	0	5
MILF	1	3
N17RO	4	1
PIJ	4	1
RIRA	0	1
SL	3	1

NOTE: Nothing in the framework precludes intermediate values (e.g., scoring a group with a capabilities level of "2.5") if there is evidence that a group's intentions or capabilities are in fact intermediate between two rungs on our scale or are on the verge of a significant change. Please see Chapter Four for more on the dynamic nature of terrorist organizations.

5 being the most hostile and 0 benign. Capabilities are similarly ranked, with 5 being the highest level of skill.[17]

Figure 2.2 demonstrates how the framework can provide analysts and policymakers with a useful lens for filtering through the chaotic noise of terrorist threats. Indeed, this paradigm clarifies the most fundamental question underlying a successful counterterrorism strategy: "What groups should the United States be worried about the most?" Figure 2.2 illustrates our answer: The terrorist groups in the upper right-hand quadrant—those that combine high levels of anti-U.S. sentiment with significant operational capabilities—should be the highest priority for U.S. counterterrorism policy. Accordingly, three groups—al Qaeda, FARC, and Hizballah—fall in this category.

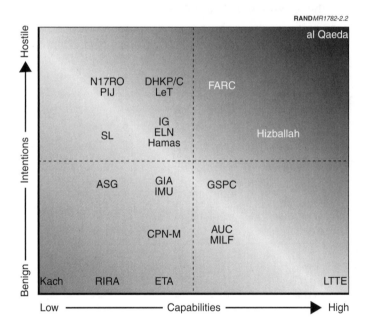

Figure 2.2—Mapping Intentions Against Capabilities for
22 Terrorist Groups

---

[17]Both the intentions and capabilities measurements are based on rhetoric and/or terrorist attacks conducted by these groups since 1998.

Although the purpose of this framework is to compare the threats posed by terrorist groups to the United States, it is important to note that *not all* of the groups in the upper right-hand quadrant are necessarily capable or motivated to launch a series of sophisticated attacks *within the United States*. It might be useful to establish a separate set of criteria specifically for attacks on the U.S. homeland, but the purpose of this analysis is to look at terrorist groups' capabilities and intentions vis-à-vis the United States *and* U.S. strategic interests abroad.

In contrast to al Qaeda, FARC, and Hizballah, terrorist groups in the lower left quadrant of the figure present the weakest threat to the United States because they have minimal degrees of both capability and desire to attack the United States. We by no means are arguing that the U.S. government should disregard these groups altogether; but rather, we recommend that policymakers weigh them in the context of ongoing strategic interests. Indeed, the United States relies on such countries as the Philippines to pursue its war on terrorism. In these circumstances, relatively incapable terrorist groups—such as the ASG—could prove to be enough of a threat that the U.S. government is compelled by the demands of coalition politics to become engaged in local (from the U.S. perspective) conflicts.

The two "extreme" quadrants—the lower left and the upper right—are the easiest to prioritize according to threats against the United States and U.S. strategic interests. Prioritizing the other two quadrants, however, is more difficult. The implication of this chapter is that terrorist threats should be prioritized both according to existing threats and to an *evaluation of how groups might change* both their motivations and their capabilities. For example, a capable terrorist group, such as the LTTE, would likely be a significant adversary if it focused on the United States. Alternatively, a hostile yet relatively incapable group, such as the Palestinian Islamic Jihad (PIJ), would likely be just as challenging if it managed to increase its capabilities to the level of the LTTE, for example.

Evaluating how terrorist groups might change, however, is not an easy task. It is a complex issue, since terrorist groups do not necessarily develop along a linear trajectory that can be mapped easily. As a result, terrorism analyses frequently focus on threats over a limited time frame, without attempting to project into the future or therefore design counterterrorism policies that might stop the evolution of groups before they reach a high threat level. In an attempt to take a first step at rectifying this shortcoming, we focus in Chapter Four on the question "What factors affect terrorist groups' development, either positively or negatively?" At this point, we acknowledge this complexity and the fact that terrorist groups are not static entities but rather ever-adapting organizations. Figure 2.3 illustrates this concept.

Figure 2.3 is not meant to predict, but rather it simply illustrates the effects that a dispersal of al Qaeda members into other terrorist groups (as a result of recent U.S. activities in Afghanistan) *might have* on the intentions and capabilities of other "affiliated" groups.

Arguably, if al Qaeda members share their technical expertise with like-minded groups, it will likely increase the groups' operational capabilities. Similarly, these groups might become more anti-U.S. as a result of al Qaeda's influence. The upward movement of the GIA and the Islamic Movement of Uzbekistan (IMU) in Figure 2.3 (solid

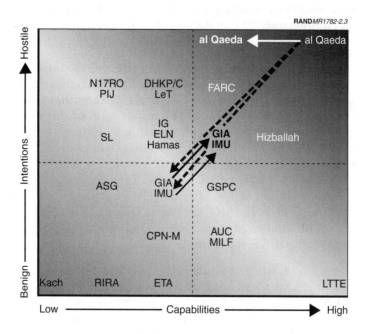

Figure 2.3—Notional Changes in Mappings as al Qaeda Cadres Migrate

black lines) illustrates this notional change, while the leftward movement of al Qaeda (solid white line) represents a potential decrease in
the organization's capabilities as a result of the war in Afghanistan.
Notably, both these shifts are only notional. The objective of Figure
2.3, at this point, is to illustrate the utility of this framework in clarify-
ing our understanding of existing and emerging terrorist threats.

Having evaluated various terrorist groups by their intentions and
capabilities, we explore what underlies these capabilities—the organizational and operational resources that sustain groups—in the next
chapter. And, more specifically, what do terrorist groups need to
survive and operate a successful campaign?

Chapter Three

TERRORIST GROUPS' CAPABILITIES

On August 7, 1998, at 10:30 a.m., a truck bomb exploded outside the U.S. embassy in Nairobi, Kenya, killing 213 people and injuring about 4,000.[1] Approximately nine minutes later, in a coordinated attack, another truck bomb killed 11 more people at the U.S. embassy in Tanzania.[2] Before and since these attacks, terrorists have kidnapped U.S. citizens, bombed U.S. businesses, and hijacked U.S. airplanes. Between 1968 and 1998, more than 3,300 terrorist attacks were conducted against U.S. targets overseas.[3] This chapter examines the tools that terrorist groups use to sustain these and other types of attacks.

HYPOTHESIZING TERRORIST TOOLS

To do this, we first divide terrorist groups' activities (and therefore requirements) into two categories:

• activities that sustain the group's existence as a cohesive entity

• activities that allow terrorists to sustain series of successful attacks.

---

[1] Bergen (2001, pp. 109–110).

[2] Bergen (2001, p. 113).

[3] The RAND Terrorism Chronology identified 3,339 attacks against U.S. targets in this period. For more information, see http://db.mipt.org.

Admittedly, these two categories are somewhat interrelated. Terrorist groups able to sustain a series of successful attacks can turn this success into a recruitment campaign or use the success to reinforce their members' confidence in the group and, hence, bolster group cohesion. Yet we chose to divide terrorist activities into these two categories because the division clarifies the potential use of, and goals for, U.S. counterterrorism policy. For example, if U.S. policymakers want to prevent a particular attack or alleviate an immediate threat, then counterterrorism activities should focus, in general, on the second category. In comparison, if policymakers want to completely dismantle a terrorist group over the long term, then counterterrorism activities should include a significant emphasis on the first category. For the purpose of this report, we have defined terrorist capabilities that sustain group cohesion and existence as *organizational tools*. Alternatively, *operational tools* provide terrorists with the capabilities necessary to sustain a series of successful attacks.[4]

Having divided terrorist groups' activities into two categories, we next identify eleven basic tools that terrorists use—with varying degrees of sophistication—to sustain these activities. The four *organizational* tools are (1) a guiding and motivating ideology, (2) leadership, (3) recruitment pools, and (4) publicity. In addition to these organizational tools, we expect that the *operational* tools used by terrorist groups to sustain a series of successful attacks are as follows: (5) command and control, (6) weapons, (7) training, (8) operational space,[5] (9) operational security, (10) intelligence, and (11) money.

To further explore these requirements, we draw observations from four terrorist groups: the RIRA, Hamas, FARC, and al Qaeda. We did not select these groups because they represent each of the four quadrants in the Chapter Two threat framework. Instead, we chose these militant groups because they appear to be indicative of other terrorist groups operating at similar levels in our *capability thresholds*, dis-

---

[4]For more information on approaches to analyzing terrorist groups, see Bonnie Cordes, Brian Michael Jenkins, Konrad Kellen, Gail V. Bass-Golod, Daniel A. Relles, William F. Sater, Mario L. Juncosa, William Fowler, and Geraldine Petty, *A Conceptual Framework for Analyzing Terrorist Groups*, Santa Monica, Calif.: RAND Corporation, R-3151, 1985.

[5]Operational space is defined in this report as the time and space to plan, train for, and execute attacks.

cussed in Chapter Two. As such, we use them as "ideal types" for terrorist groups operating at four of the five different capability levels included in our framework. Although subsequent sections describe the capabilities of these groups in more detail, the following provides a brief background on their motivations, modus operandi, and operating environments.

The RIRA is a terrorist group that operates primarily in Northern Ireland. Its supporters are referred to as *Republicans* because they support a unification of Northern Ireland with the Republic of Ireland. Leaders of the PIRA, the RIRA's parent organization, entered into peace negotiations with the British government in 1998. Some PIRA fighters rejected this peace process, however, and split from the PIRA to establish their own terrorist group and to continue to fight against British authorities. The RIRA was founded by the PIRA's ex-quartermaster general Michael McKevitt and his common-law wife Bernadette Sands-McKevitt, who together recruited several of the PIRA's skilled bombmakers into the organization, giving the group a tremendous operational advantage. Sands-McKevitt's participation also gave the group credibility within the broader Nationalist movement because she was the sister of Bobby Sands, the first PIRA member to die in a hunger strike in 1981.[6] Most of the RIRA's attacks are comprised of relatively low-level operations, such as riots, bombs left outside an opponent's home, or beatings. One of the most sophisticated attacks conducted by the group was an August 1998 car bombing in Omagh, which killed 28 people and injured about 100.[7] Thus, the RIRA represents the least capable group in our analysis (capability level 1 in Table 2.4).

Like the RIRA, Hamas is also a rejectionist group, opposing Palestinian negotiations with Israel and the Oslo Accords. Yet in contrast to the RIRA, which is motivated primarily by a nationalist agenda, Hamas also has a religious objective: an Islamic state in Palestine.[8]

---

[6] "Paramilitaries: The Real IRA/32-County Sovereignty Committee," British Broadcasting Corporation, www.bbc.co.uk/history/war/troubles/factfiles/rira.shtml (accessed September 2003).

[7] For more information on the Real IRA, see Sean Boyne, "The Real IRA: After Omagh, What Now?" *Jane's Intelligence Review*, August 24, 1998.

[8] For more information on Hamas, see Khaled Hroub, *Hamas: Political Thought and Practice*, Washington, D.C.: Institute for Palestine Studies, 2000.

Like other terrorist groups in the region, such as Egypt's al Gamat, Hamas's ideological roots are planted firmly in the Muslim Brotherhood. Thus, Hamas uses suicide bombings to challenge both Israel and the secular government promoted by the Palestinian Authority in the West Bank and Gaza Strip. Hamas represents approximately one level above the RIRA in capabilities, or capability level 2 in Table 2.4.

FARC is a guerrilla organization that sometimes uses terrorist tactics to achieve its goals. As such, it is a much larger group (approximately 15,000 members) than Hamas, maintaining control over people and territory in Colombia, as well as some small areas in Panama and Ecuador. FARC articulates a Marxist-Leninist agenda—e.g., land reforms, redistribution of power and wealth—and yet this agenda now incorporates drug trafficking.[9] Operationally, FARC often kidnaps international and local businessmen, holding them for ransom. It also attacks bridges, military installations, and utilities; conducts car bombings in Colombia's major cities; and plots assassinations of government officials. We ranked FARC as "3" on the capability indicators in Table 2.4.[10]

Finally, al Qaeda's leadership has articulated multiple objectives: remove U.S. influence from the Gulf States, eliminate corruption in Saudi Arabia, kill numerous Americans, and reestablish the Caliphate.[11] Al Qaeda's agenda, therefore, encompasses much broader objectives than the other three groups. Similarly, it has demonstrated the ability to promote its agenda on a global scale. Its repertoire of attacks include the September 11, 2001, attacks on the

---

[9]For a discussion of FARC, see Angel Rabasa and Peter Chalk, *The Colombian Labyrinth: The Synergy of Drugs and Insurgency and Its Implications for Regional Stability*, Santa Monica, Calif.: RAND Corporation, MR-1339-AF, 2001.

[10]Note that our discussion of FARC focuses primarily on its terrorist capabilities, not guerrilla warfare tactics.

[11]The Caliphate is used, generally, to refer to the people and lands ruled by the spiritual head of the theocratic Islamic state. Many Sunnis regard the period of the first four Caliphs after Mohammed—Abu Bakr, Umar, Uthman, and Ali—as the Islamic ideal. One of the primary objectives of al Qaeda is to overthrow the existing secular Arab governments and replace them with a truly Islamic nation.

For a discussion of al Qaeda and its objectives, see Anonymous, *Through Our Enemies' Eyes*, Washington, D.C.: Brassey's, 2002, pp. 45–73, and Bergen (2001).

World Trade Center and the Pentagon; a maritime attack on the USS *Cole* in Yemen; suicide truck bombings in Kenya, Tanzania, and Tunisia; and planned attacks on NATO ships in the Straits of Gibraltar and on the U.S. embassy in Rome. Thus, we ranked al Qaeda as "5" on the capability indicators in Table 2.2. Two levels above FARC, al Qaeda represents the most capable group in our analysis.

The next section uses observations of these four terrorist groups to explore groups' organizational and operational requirements. The chapter then concludes with a discussion of the resulting vulnerabilities exposed by terrorist groups and their implications for U.S. counterterrorism strategy.

ORGANIZATIONAL TOOLS

As mentioned previously, we expect the four, broadly defined organizational requirements for terrorist groups to be ideology, leadership, recruitment pools, and publicity. Thus, all four of the case studies in this analysis—the RIRA, Hamas, FARC, and al Qaeda—should rely on these tools to keep their organizations functioning as a cohesive unit. The following sections explore each of the organizational requirements as they relate to these four terrorist groups.

Ideology

With regards to terrorism, the term *ideology*[12] means the consensus of grievances and objectives that a terrorist group is trying to address through violence.[13] In this context, terrorists' ideologies may take on many forms—e.g., religious or political—but still serve the same pur-

---

[12]We decided to address ideology as a key organizational tool because it helps cement group cohesion. In many cases, terrorist groups use their ideology as an instrument in a struggle for power vis-à-vis state governments. Cohesion also plays a role in sustaining the terrorist organization itself.

[13]Sidney Tarrow discusses the necessity for consensus mobilization within nonviolent and violent social movements. In the same way, terrorist organizations often draw from these wider social movements in justifying their own ideology. (*Power in Movement: Social Movements, Collective Action and Politics*, Cambridge, United Kingdom: Cambridge University Press, 1994, pp. 118–134)

pose—motivating actions, unifying members, and linking the organization to communities for which it purports to fight.[14]

The RIRA appears to follow the pattern discussed above. As mentioned previously, its members continue to fight to free Northern Ireland from British rule and unify it with the Republic of Ireland. Moreover, most of the RIRA's members are former PIRA fighters, articulating the same basic objectives of Northern Ireland's independence from England and its unification with the Republic of Ireland.[15] As a result, it is fairly easy for the RIRA to maintain group cohesion because it draws on a long precedent of Republican ideology that has, similarly, served to motivate political violence for almost a century. The ideological link between the RIRA and its support community, however, is more tenuous. Most Republicans in Northern Ireland support the peace efforts advocated by the Social and Democratic Labor Party (SDLP) and Sinn Fein (PIRA's political branch).[16] Yet because the RIRA is a small group (approximately 100 members), it does not need an extensive support community; therefore, this third role of ideology may be less important to the survival of the group.[17]

Of course, it is not always easy to categorize the ideology of a particular group. Hamas sees its terrorist campaign against Israel as part of the fight for Palestinian independence. But the organization is also locked in a religious struggle within the Palestinian establishment it-

---

[14]For further discussion on the role of collective rationale and identity in terrorism, see Martha Crenshaw, "The Logic of Terrorism: Terrorist Behavior as a Product of Strategic Choice," and Albert Bandura, "Mechanisms of Moral Disengagement," in Walter Reich, *Origins of Terrorism*, Washington, D.C.: Woodrow Wilson Center Press, 1998, pp. 7–24, 161–191.

[15]For more information on the PIRA and terrorism in Northern Ireland, see Tim Pat Coogan, *The Troubles: Ireland's Ordeal, 1965–1995, and the Search for Peace*, London: Hutchinson, 1995. For further discussion on the RIRA, see James Dingley, "The Bombing on Omagh, 15 August 1998: The Bombers, Their Tactics, Strategy and Purpose Behind the Incident," *Studies in Conflict and Terrorism*, No. 24, 2001, pp. 451–465.

[16]For more information on the Belfast Agreement and peace process, see "Ulster Peace: How Fragile?" *New York Times*, February 3, 1995; "Britain and Ireland Issue a Plan for Full Talks on Ulster," *New York Times*, February 23, 1995; and the Belfast Agreement, accessible online at www.ofmdfmni.gov.uk/publications/ba.htm (accessed September 2003).

[17]Dingley (2001, pp. 451–465).

self, against the proponents of a secular state.[18] As such, Hamas has to balance its religious and nationalist ideologies to maintain group cohesion. To do this, the terrorist group allows its members to participate in local elections in the West Bank and Gaza Strip, yet it does not sponsor candidates for the Legislative Council.[19] By adopting this strategy, Hamas is able to sustain its nationalist ideology without legitimizing the establishment of a *secular* Palestinian state. Although its ideology is more complex than that of the RIRA, Hamas still appears to use it to motivate actions, unify members, and link the group to Palestinian supporters in the West Bank and Gaza Strip.

In contrast, FARC engages in guerrilla warfare and its ideology is neither nationalist nor religious; instead, it claims to fight for control of Colombia to take power and institute socialist reforms.[20] FARC can, therefore, be viewed as having an insurgent strategy as well as a radical socialist ideology. Moreover, it is the combination of both ideology and strategy in this case that galvanizes its members toward a common goal. So although this pattern is different than that of the RIRA and Hamas, we believe that it is close enough to still fit within the *basic pattern of ideology*. However, in addition, FARC and its support communities are heavily engaged in the illegal drug trade.[21] This involvement confounds the role that ideology plays for FARC, and it becomes difficult to tell if FARC members support the objectives of the group or the drug economy. So far, FARC has not faced a substantial conflict of interests between these two factors, but the issue of drugs may eventually erode its ideological base.

Finally, as mentioned above, al Qaeda's leaders have commingled religious and political strains within its ideology. Al Qaeda does this because it pulls its leaders and operatives from multiple terrorist groups, each with its own particular set of local objectives. Al Qaeda then unites these multiple objectives under a pan-Islamic ideology,

---

[18]Ziad Abu-Amr, *Islamic Fundamentalism in the West Bank and Gaza*, Bloomington, Ind.: Indiana University Press, 1994, pp. 128–129.

[19]Shaul Mishal and Avraham Sela, *The Palestinian Hamas*, New York: Columbia University Press, 2000, pp. 13–55, 76.

[20]For a basic overview of FARC, see Brian Michael Jenkins, "Colombia: Crossing a Dangerous Threshold," *The National Interest,* Winter 2000, pp. 47–55.

[21]For further discussion, see Rabasa and Chalk (2001).

presenting the different groups with a common enemy: the United States.[22] Of course, this coalescence is not simply due to ideology; other factors have contributed to al Qaeda's success. The following sections examine some of these additional factors.[23]

Leadership

Leadership represents our second organizational tool (note that we are not discussing requirements in any particular hierarchical order). In this instance, leadership is different than the command and control requirements of a particular operation. For example, in *Insurgency and Terrorism*, Bard O'Neill observes that terrorist groups tend to coalesce around charismatic individuals who attract and inspire supporters.[24] Therefore, leadership in this context plays a more cohesive than operational role, and we would expect that all four of the groups in this analysis evidence fairly charismatic leaders.

Michael McKevitt founded and led the RIRA until his arrest in March 2001. Because of his previous leadership role within the PIRA, McKevitt was able to recruit members from the ranks of the PIRA and form a cohesive group relatively easily.[25] Similarly, McKevitt drew on his relationship (through marriage) to former PIRA hero Bobby Sands to solidify his and his group's legitimacy in the Republican movement.[26] Since his arrest, the RIRA has continued to operate, but there has been some dissension in the group. In October 2002, UK newspapers reported the establishment of a potential new breakaway faction inside the RIRA.[27] The experience of the RIRA, therefore, appears to follow the pattern of needing a charismatic leader to maintain group cohesion.

---

[22]Anonymous (2002, pp. 170–182).

[23]Anonymous (2002, pp. 45–68, 169–182).

[24]Bard O'Neill, *Insurgency and Terrorism: Inside Modern Revolutionary Warfare*, Washington, D.C.: Brassey's, 1990, p. 75.

[25]Dingley (2001, p. 476).

[26]"Corkman in Charge as Real IRA Threat Remains," *Irish Times*, May 24, 2001.

[27]Rosie Cowan, "Real IRA 'Ready to Attack Again,'" *Guardian Unlimited*, October 21, 2002.

Similarly, Sheikh Yassin serves as the spiritual leader for Hamas.[28] As mentioned above, Hamas has its ideological roots in Egypt's Muslim Brotherhood. Although the Islamic movement developed and expanded in the Occupied Territories as early as the 1970s, Hamas and its militant wing, the al-Qassam Martyrs Brigades, were not established until the *intifada*.[29] To establish the group, Yassin was able to use his charisma and legitimacy as an Islamic scholar to draw recruits from the refugee camps in the West Bank and Gaza.[30] Currently, Hamas has other political leaders as well as military leaders in both the West Bank and Gaza Strip. Yet Yassin apparently still provides a unifying center for all the different components of Hamas: political, economic, and military.

FARC represents a similar pattern, but one distributed over a wider range of members and territory. Manual Marulanda functions as the charismatic center of the organization, providing overall ideological and motivational guidance.[31] Yet substantial operational control remains in the hands of individuals who command FARC's various "fronts."[32] Although FARC frequently brings these commanders together for organizationwide coordination meetings, it is logical to assume that many members of FARC have not met and are not loyal to Marulanda personally, but rather the leaders of their fronts.[33] As such, these front commanders play an essential role in maintaining group cohesion.

Finally, while Osama bin Laden apparently remains al Qaeda's ideological and inspirational leader, the organization's affiliated groups still rely on their various leaders to maintain unity within al Qaeda. Many of the terrorist groups allegedly affiliated with al Qaeda, such as the Moro Islamic Liberation Front (MILF) in the Philippines, recruit members and conduct attacks without oversight from al

---

[28]Hroub (2000, pp. 209–251).

[29]Mishal and Sela (2000, pp. 18, 55–64).

[30]Mishal and Sela (2000, pp. 16–20).

[31]For more information, see "El Voto de Tirofijo," *Semana*, June 29, 1998, pp. 24–28.

[32]For examples, see "Armas por Coca," *Cambio*, July 12, 1999, p. 30.

[33]For more information, see "Los Planes de las Farc," *Semana*, August 7, 2000, p. 35.

Qaeda.[34] This pattern is, therefore, similar to that of FARC but is on a global scale and across multiple groups.

Admittedly, leadership is a key issue in counterterrorism policy, and this section would benefit from a more extensive examination of other terrorist groups' leaders; however, our research shows that *leadership* is significantly more complex than we originally hypothesized.[35] While the experience of the RIRA might indicate that targeting terrorist leaders would destroy group cohesion, Hamas, FARC, and al Qaeda seem to have enough midlevel leaders—with their own command of loyalty—to absorb the loss of a core leader. We conclude, therefore, that *leadership's* role in maintaining group cohesion depends as much on the structure of the organization (multiple or single layers of leaders) as it does on one leader's charisma.

Recruitment Pools

Recruitment pools are one of the most important requirements for terrorist groups to survive over time. Groups need new members both to grow in strength and to replenish losses and defections. Recruitment can be so important that one study of left-wing terrorism in Italy from 1970 to 1983 found that groups conducted increasingly lethal attacks, in part, to gain more recruits.[36] We therefore

---

[34]The MILF was established as a splinter movement of the Moro National Liberation Front (MNLF) in 1977. The group is led by Hashim Salamat, and its political objective is the establishment of an Islamic state in the areas where Muslims constitute a majority in the southern Philippines. For more information, see "Tide of Insurgency in South East Asia," *Jane's Terrorism and Security Monitor*, May 1, 2000.

[35]The two cases most often cited as examples of how eliminating leaders can have a deleterious effect on a terrorist group are the removal of Abiemael Guzmán from the SL in Peru and Abdullah Ocalan from the Kurdistan Workers' Party (PKK) in Turkey. Other cases, such as the death of Hizballah leaders, have not had a disastrous effect on their respective groups. Interestingly, in both the Guzmán and Ocalan cases, the structure of the organization was such that no clear succession plan existed, which is not the same for the other, contrasting groups. This indicates that more factors were involved in the dissolution of the SL and the PKK than simply the removal of their leaders.

[36]See Donatella della Porta "Left-Wing Terrorism in Italy," in Martha Crenshaw, ed., *Terrorism in Context*, State College, Pa.: Pennsylvania State University Press, 1995, pp. 134–137, 157.

expect that the RIRA, Hamas, FARC, and al Qaeda expend considerable resources on recruitment activities.

Functioning as a small terrorist cell, the RIRA originally drew most of its recruits from the ranks of former PIRA fighters. This recruitment allowed the RIRA to begin its activities with an immediate pool of hardened operators, already skilled at building bombs and avoiding British authorities. In addition, other reports suggest that the RIRA attempts to recruit young persons without a past record of violent activities, in such areas as south Armagh, Derry, and Dublin.[37] Furthermore, it appears that these new recruits support the breakaway faction.[38] If such reports are true, the case of the RIRA illustrates not only the importance that terrorist groups place on new recruits to sustain their existence but also the dangers involved in not integrating recruits in such a way that they bolster group cohesion.

Hamas has also concentrated considerable time and resources on its potential recruitment pools. As mentioned above, Yassin originally pulled his supporters from refugee camps in the West Bank and Gaza Strip, but Hamas now also recruits from local universities and prisons.[39] Indeed, Hamas has strengthened its ties to communities that hold potential recruits through its support for social institutions, such as educational institutions (kindergartens through universities), orphanages, health clinics, and sport clubs, in the Occupied Territories.[40] Some reports indicate that Hamas spends up to 60 percent of its income on these and other social-type activities.[41] Moreover, Hamas has been known to put new recruits through months-long probationary periods, during which already-members indoctrinate them in an effort to both evaluate and strengthen their loyalty.[42] Thus Hamas, like the RIRA, views recruitment pools as a key organi-

---

[37]Boyne (1998); Cowan (2002).

[38]"Corkman in Charge as Real IRA Threat Remains" (2001); Cowan (2002).

[39]Abu-Amr (1994, pp. 92–94).

[40]Hroub (2000, pp. 36–41, 235–242).

[41]Johanna McGeary, "Hamas: Popular, Extreme, and an Alternative to Arafat," *Time*, Vol. 158, No. 26, December 17, 2001, p. 54.

[42]David Van Biema, "Why the Bombers Keep Coming," *Time*, Vol. 158, No. 26, December 17, 2001, p. 54.

zational requirement and invests considerable time and resources in sustaining these pools.

Historically, FARC has drawn its members from *campesinos,* peasants living primarily in Colombia's rural southwest.[43] As it began to expand its activities in the early 1990s, FARC attempted to recruit new members through conscription and intimidation tactics.[44] This strategy was also in response to pressure from the Self-Defense Forces of Colombia (AUC), which was not only fighting against FARC but competing with it for recruits and resources as well.[45] From 1998 to 2001, FARC and the AUC fought for control over people and territory in the drug-producing areas of Colombia and along its major trafficking corridors. This fight was brutal, as militants from both groups slaughtered villagers in retaliatory attacks on their opponent's supporters. If FARC's experience follows the pattern of other terrorist groups, such as the SL in Peru, it is likely that this brutality will reduce local support for FARC in areas that have historically provided it with recruits, thus weakening group solidarity and the organization's ability to recruit operatives.[46]

Finally, al Qaeda appears to recruit its members on multiple levels. For example, the organization recruits and trains operatives for specific attacks, as in the case of the "Hamburg cell" and its role in the September 11 attacks. In this instance, potential recruits were identified and observed over a period of one to two years and then brought to Afghanistan for further observation and training.[47] In

---

[43]Marc Chernick, "Negotiating Peace Amid Multiple Forms of Violence," in Cynthia Arnson, ed., *Comparative Peace Processes in Latin America,* Washington, D.C.: Woodrow Wilson Center Press, 1999, pp. 164–172.

[44]"Army Reports Heavy Child Involvement in Guerrilla War," *El País,* December 27, 2000.

[45]"Army Reports Heavy Child Involvement in Guerrilla War"(2000); Scott Wilson, "Interview with Carlos Castano, Head of the United Self-Defense Forces of Colombia," *Washington Post,* March 12, 2001.

[46]See Chapter Four for more information on the Shining Path and its relationship to its support communities in the 1990s.

[47]For more information on the Hamburg cell, see "Man Alleged to Aid 9/11 Cell Arrested in German Inquiry: Moroccan Man Assisted Hamburg Group, Officials Say," *Washington Post,* October 11, 2002; "Traces of Terror: Sept. 11 Attacks Planned in '99, Germans Learn," *New York Times,* August 30, 2002; and "Clerics May Have Stoked

other circumstances, al Qaeda relies on the members of local groups with similar ideologies and goals to act as its "recruits," as in the case of the October 2002 bombing in Bali.[48] Therefore, al Qaeda appears to recruit local foot soldiers as well as individuals with specific skills and characteristics (e.g., having passports from Western countries), depending on its planned attacks. This pattern and degree of sophistication is, at this point, isolated to al Qaeda.

Our analysis therefore indicates that, although recruitment pools *are* a requirement for terrorist groups at all capability levels, the manifestation of this requirement varies according to the group's organizational structure and support communities.

Publicity

Publicity—media attention and direct external communications—is the final tool in our list of organizational requirements. Publicity enables groups to promote their ideology, advertise their accomplishments, and otherwise get their message out to various audiences. Historically, terrorist groups have appealed to three primary audiences: their own members, supporters outside the group, and adversaries and other observers.[49] This section examines the efforts made by RIRA, Hamas, FARC, and al Qaeda leaders to convince supporters that their group is actually "doing something" to achieve its goals.

Both the RIRA and Hamas have historically claimed their attacks, either in calls to media outlets or locally distributed leaflets.[50] Hamas also uses its websites to promote the actions of its martyrs and showcase oppressive Israeli acts.[51] Hamas's strategy has two prongs: to

---

Radicals' Fire: Qaeda Said to Use Some Radical Clerics to Help Its Cause," *Boston Globe*, August 4, 2002.

[48]"What If He Isn't Guilty?" *Far Eastern Economic Review*, November 7, 2002; "Weak Link in the Anti-Terror Chain," *Far Eastern Economic Review*, October 24, 2002.

[49]Hoffman (1998, pp. 131–136).

[50]For the RIRA, see "The Real IRA Split as Warning Is Given," *Guardian Unlimited*, October 22, 2002, and for Hamas see Mishal and Sela (2000, pp. 75–77).

[51]The Hamas website can be accessed at www.palestine-info.net. There are also reports that some groups are using the Internet for command and control purposes. Al Qaeda, for example, is alleged to have used chat rooms to pass instructions and other

use terrorism to destabilize the Israeli government, and to challenge the Palestinian Authority. Similarly, the RIRA is still confronting the role of British authorities (primarily the Royal Ulster Constabulary) in Northern Ireland. At the same time, the organization is also challenging the "peaceful" Republican groups, such as the SDLP and Sinn Fein.

Unlike the RIRA or Hamas, FARC's leaders do not consistently take credit in the local media for their attacks. Yet FARC does maintain approximately 14 of its own radio transmitting stations, known as the "Bolivarian Radio Network," which helps the group communicate with its members in the large area under its control. One of these stations, "Voice of the Resistance," transmits FARC propaganda, recruitment messages, and popular local music.[52] Although this pattern is slightly different than that of the RIRA or Hamas, it is consistent with FARC's insurgent strategy. Moreover, Colombian authorities tend to attribute most of the violence in the country to FARC, so the organization does not necessarily need to make extra effort to draw attention to its activities.

Like FARC, al Qaeda has not historically claimed its attacks, at least in the case of the 1998 embassy bombings, the USS *Cole* attack, or the September 11 attacks. However, recent tapes obtained by Arab media outlets indicate that al Qaeda members do record martyrdom messages.[53] These videos allow al Qaeda to demonstrate the determination of its members to the Muslim world as well as to its adversaries. Similarly, al Qaeda leaders have delivered messages to media outlets, such as al-Jazeera or al-Manar, referencing recent attacks and encouraging audiences to continue their support.[54]

---

information to and among operatives. For more information, see Paul Eedle, "Al-Qaeda Takes Fight for 'Hearts and Minds' to the Web," *Jane's Intelligence Review*, August 1, 2002, and Jack Kelley, "Militants Wire Web with Links to Jihad Islamic Groups," *Newsfactor.com*, July 10, 2002.

[52]Juan Tamayo, "Colombia's FARC Has a CD, Too," *Miami Herald*, August 13, 2001.

[53]Kevin Johnson and Toni Locy, "Men on Tapes Seem Ready to Die for Al-Qaeda," *USA Today*, January 18, 2002; Eedle (2002).

[54]For more information on al-Jazeera or other media in the Middle East, see Mohammed el-Nawawy and Adel Iskandar, *Al-Jazeera: How the Free Arab News Network Scooped the World and Changed the Middle East*, Cambridge, Mass.: Westview Press, 2002, and Dale F. Eickelman and Jon W. Anderson, eds., *New Media in the Muslim World*, Bloomington, Ind.: Indiana University Press, 1999.

Observations on Organizational Tools

We can draw two general observations from the section above: Terrorist groups' needs for ideology and publicity remain fairly consistent across organizations of differing capabilities, and leadership and recruitment are more sensitive to variations in organizational structure and dynamics between the terrorists and their support communities. Leadership is one organizational requirement that may be susceptible to immediate counterterrorism activities. Yet, this appears to be true only for groups without a dynamic structure, which allows for promotion and the development of midlevel leaders. Similarly, our research suggests that counterterrorism efforts focusing on recruitment are likely to have a more significant impact on larger, more-dispersed organizations, especially in the long term.[55]

In fact, organizational dynamics and support communities appear to be underlying themes for all four of the instruments discussed in this section. Furthermore, understanding these themes can structure future ways of thinking about counterterrorism policy. Specifically, this section has implications for the potential prospects of counterterrorism policies that attempt to delegitimize ideologies, eliminate leaders, dry up recruitment pools, and reduce terrorists' access to their audiences. We conclude that, although terrorists' reliance on leadership and recruitment pools show the most variety, they are also likely to be the most vulnerable to counterterrorism activities.

OPERATIONAL TOOLS

This section begins with the hypothesis that terrorist groups need seven "operational" tools to sustain a series of successful attacks: command and control, weapons, operational space, operational security, training, intelligence, and money. Similar to the previous

---

[55]Notably, this analysis examines only four terrorist groups. Because these groups represent different strengths, organizational structures, ideologies and environmental surroundings, we argue that any findings drawn from similarities among them are fairly significant. However, it is clear that further research could be conducted to either support or refute these preliminary findings—particularly the assertion that counterterrorism efforts that focus on recruitment are more likely to have a significant impact on larger, more-dispersed organizations in the long term.

section, we expect that these requirements will follow a consistent pattern for the RIRA, Hamas, FARC, and al Qaeda. Furthermore, we expect these tools to bolster the groups' ability to *conduct attacks*, as opposed to sustaining group cohesion.

Command and Control

For the purpose of this report, *command and control* is the mechanism that terrorist groups use to plan, coordinate, and execute their attacks. Notably, terrorist leaders often attempt to build a degree of redundancy into their command and control network in order to coordinate activities. However, this redundancy also increases the risk of leaks or penetrations.[56] Thus, we expect that all four terrorist groups examined here would attempt to sustain a command and control network for their activities as well as protect networks from infiltration.

Because the RIRA is a small group with members concentrated in a relatively limited area, command and control requirements for attacks are similarly limited. Yet, despite this relative benefit of a small group, the RIRA still has some command and control difficulties, primarily as a result of the counterterrorism successes of British authorities. For example, in September 2002, British authorities arrested two RIRA terrorists attempting to plant bombs in Newry, which brought the total number of the group's prisoners to 46.[57] Thus, it appears that authorities continue to use infiltrators and informers effectively to arrest RIRA leaders and disrupt its command and control network, thereby interrupting the momentum of the group's activities.

Similarly, Hamas's command and control requirements in the early 1990s were minimal: The group relied on leaflets and couriers to co-

---

[56]For further discussion, see G. H. McCormick and G. Gown, "Security and Coordination in Clandestine Organization," *Mathematical and Computer Modelling*, No. 31, 2000, pp. 175–192, as well as J. Bowyer Bell, "Revolutionary Dynamics: The Inherent Inefficiency of the Underground," *Terrorism and Political Violence*, Vol. 2, No. 4, 1990, pp. 193–211.

[57]Cowan (2002).

ordinate operations.[58] However, recent reports indicate that Hamas has adjusted its command and control network to account for its expanding influence and Israeli counterterrorism activities during the ongoing al-Aqsa intifada. Hamas now has operational commands in the West Bank and Gaza Strip, with "replacement teams" for upcoming operations in case members are assassinated or arrested by Israeli security forces.[59] This structure allows Hamas to protect its word-of-mouth command and control network and to reduce the risk that Israeli counterterrorism activities will interrupt the momentum of its attacks.

FARC's command and control network consists of a hierarchy of midlevel leaders who meet periodically to formulate basic strategic guidance, allowing the leaders discretion in the way that they achieve their overall objectives.[60] This network is then further facilitated by a system of radio transmitting stations, as discussed above. Moreover, from 1998 to 2002, FARC operated within a demilitarized zone (DMZ) in southwestern Colombia. This DMZ allowed FARC members to coordinate their activities relatively openly, without concern for overt arrest or disruption. However, FARC's network does have some vulnerabilities, and disconnects have appeared between the group's top leaders and midlevel commanders. For example, in February 2000, FARC members kidnapped and killed nine hikers in Colombia's Purace National Park, apparently without the prior knowledge or consent of the group's political leaders.[61] This resulted in turmoil within the FARC and a backlash from the group's traditional supporters who were outraged by the attack.[62]

Al Qaeda has also developed a decentralized command and control system, albeit on a wider, global scale. Like FARC, al Qaeda apparently allows substantial autonomy to individual local groups. These

---

[58]Some of these leaflets can be read in English in Shaul Mishal, *Speaking Stones,* Syracuse, N.Y.: Syracuse University Press, 1994.

[59]McGeary (2001, p. 52).

[60]In August 2000, *Semana,* a news journal in Colombia, published the agenda of such an annual meeting. For more information, see "Los Planes de las Farc" (2000, p. 35).

[61]U.S. Department of State, Bureau of Democracy, Human Rights, and Labor, "Country Reports Human Rights Practices: 2001," March 4, 2002.

[62]U.S. Department of State (2002).

affiliated groups, such as the MILF in the Philippines or the Jemaah Islamiya in Indonesia, conduct many terrorist operations without specific guidance from al Qaeda. Yet when members of al Qaeda's "hard core" decide to conduct a specific attack, its cells located around the world—in Sudan, Turkey, Spain, the United Kingdom, Germany, Yemen, and elsewhere—rely on the leaders of these affiliated groups to help support and coordinate their activities.[63] In the past, al Qaeda's planning cells also traveled to and from safe locations, such as Afghanistan or Malaysia, for higher-level coordination meetings.[64] As a result of the loss of its safe haven in Afghanistan, al Qaeda might not rely as much on these physical meetings to sustain its command and control network. Reports by U.S. officials also indicate that al Qaeda has made use of the Internet to facilitate its global command and control network.[65]

We conclude from this analysis that command and control is a relatively consistent requirement across all terrorist groups, despite varying degrees of capabilities. Although FARC and al Qaeda attempt to maintain their networks on a wider scale, the relative difference in requirements between the four groups appears to be minor: Couriers, leaflets, radio communications, and the Internet, for example, all serve to form a loose command and control network for terrorists' operations.

Weapons

Since 1968, terrorists have employed a wide range of weapons, from knives to assault rifles to toxic chemicals. Yet, despite this variety, explosives still remain the most common weapon used by terrorist groups. From April 2001 to April 2002, approximately 60 percent of terrorist attacks worldwide included the use of bombs or other explosive devices.[66] Weapons represent a fairly logical operational

---

[63]For examples, see Anonymous (2002, pp. 134–137, 180–182, 236–240).

[64]Gunaratna (2002, p. 95).

[65]"Al-Qaeda May Use Internet to Regroup," *BBC News*, March 6, 2002.

[66]This number (which comprises 958 bombings and 74 suicide bombings out of 1,637 terrorist attacks) is taken from the RAND-MIPT Terrorism Incident Database, which can be accessed online at http://db.mipt.org.

requirement, and we expect that all four groups in this study expend resources to maintain an arsenal of weapons for their attacks.

Both the RIRA and Hamas use relatively unsophisticated weapons and, similarly, rely on local stockpiles and sources. For example, Michael McKevitt, founder of the RIRA, was in charge of maintaining the PIRA's weapon stockpiles and therefore provided his members with easy access to explosive devices and assault rifles.[67] Similarly, Hamas and other Palestinian terrorist groups have access to weapons through black market activities, including Israeli smugglers and, allegedly, Palestinian security forces.[68] Having said that, reports indicate that local sources of weapons in Israel and the Occupied Territories may not be enough to support the terrorist activities of groups in the region. Indeed, in recent attacks (fall 2002), Palestinian groups have tended to use improvised explosives; moreover, it appears that Hizballah is attempting to augment Palestinian terrorists' weapon supplies from its own caches.[69]

In contrast to Hamas and the RIRA, FARC has historically used improvised devices for its attacks, including gas canisters filled with explosives.[70] However, FARC also maintains a fairly sophisticated smuggling network of assault rifles that accesses illegal weapons supplies in both Central and South America. Finally, FARC has also reportedly attempted to acquire man-portable surface-to-air missiles.[71] If true, these weapons would help FARC in its attacks on the Colombian military, especially against counternarcotics helicopters. Yet, at the time of this study, FARC had not used any such weapons against its adversaries in Colombia.

Finally, al Qaeda has used a wide range of weapons to conduct its attacks, including car bombs, suicide bombers in maritime attacks,

---

[67]Boyne (1998); Dingley (2001, p. 476).

[68]Michael R. Gordon, "U.S. Is Given Papers That Israelis Assert Tie Arafat to Terror," *New York Times*, April 11, 2002, p. A1; "The Old West Comes to Israel," *Asia Times*, November 16, 2002.

[69]McGeary (2001, p. 52).

[70]Jared Kotler, "Guerrillas to Study Curbing the Use of Homemade Missiles," Associated Press, February 13, 2001.

[71]"Los Misiles de las Farc," *Semana*, September 6, 1999, pp. 20–24.

and passenger airplanes. Al Qaeda had been able to sustain this diversity, in part, because of its training facilities in Afghanistan. Similarly, it is likely that its connections to various terrorist groups with access to black markets in Kashmir, Central Asia, and Southeast Asia also allow its affiliates continued access to weapon supplies. Therefore, it appears that weapons are indeed an important operational requirement.

It is impossible to examine *weapons* without discussing chemical, biological, radiological, or nuclear weapons. Some terrorist groups have sought, and in a handful of cases attempted to employ, biological and chemical weapons. For example, in 1984, the Rajneeshee cult poisoned salad bars in Oregon with *Salmonella typhimurium* in an attempt to prevent group opponents from voting in a local election.[72] Similarly, members of the Algerian nonaligned mujahideen, who may have been allied with al Qaeda, manufactured the potent biotoxin ricin in a UK safe house in January 2003, potentially planning to use it to conduct a terrorist attack in the United Kingdom.[73] The LTTE used chlorine stolen from a nearby plant to release chemical fumes over a Sri Lankan armed forces base that the group attacked in 1990.[74] And Aum Shinrikyo apparently invested millions of dollars in pursuit of biological and chemical weapons, culminating in the 1995 nerve gas attack on the Tokyo subway system.[75] More specifically, with regard to the groups examined in this study, FARC's use of gas canisters filled with explosives as well as shrapnel contaminated with feces could be considered lower-level "toxic chemical" attacks; al Qaeda also has experimented with chemical substances.[76]

---

[72]Jessica Stern, *The Ultimate Terrorists*, Cambridge, Mass.: Harvard University Press, 1999, p. 67.

[73]Nick Hopkins and Tania Branigan, "Poison Find Sparks Terror Alert," *Guardian Unlimited*, January 8, 2003.

[74]Bruce Hoffman, "The Debate Over Future Terrorist Use of Chemical, Biological, Radiological, and Nuclear Weapons," in Brad Roberts, ed., *Hype or Reality? The "New Terrorism" and Mass Casualty Attacks*, Alexandria, Va.: Chemical and Biological Arms Control Institute, 2000, pp. 215–218.

[75]Stern (1999, pp. 60–68); Richard Falkenrath et al., *America's Achilles' Heel: Nuclear, Biological, and Chemical Terrorism and Covert Attack*, Cambridge, Mass.: MIT Press, 1998, pp. 19–26.

[76]"Tapes Shed New Light on Bin Laden's Network," *CNN.com*, August 19, 2002.

In sum, while *weapons,* in a general sense, constitute a logical and straightforward requirement, *access to external weapon sources* appears to be the underlying requirement for terrorist groups that operate at fairly high capability levels. Similarly, *unconventional weapons* add another degree of complexity to this requirement. Indeed, it appears that as groups expand their activities, the *reliability* of weapon supplies becomes a more important operational requirement than simply having access to large weapons stockpiles. Moreover, unconventional weapons appear to be less of a requirement for terrorist groups as they are an added benefit. These weapons are desirable for certain groups, such as Aum Shinrikyo, that have latched on to CBRN materials, or are advantageous for groups that already have a reliable source of conventional weapons. Alternatively, some groups, such as al Qaeda, may believe that CBRN weapons also have an intrinsic value and thus may consider it an imperative to acquire them.[77]

Operational Space

In addition to command and control network and weapons, terrorist groups also need time and space to plan, train for, and execute their attacks. Although we expect that this operational space will range from urban neighborhoods to state sanctuaries, the four groups discussed here all rely on the active and passive support of communities—local, national, and transnational.

The RIRA operates in a relatively constrained and urban environment in Northern Ireland and maintains a limited presence in cities outside Northern Ireland, such as Dublin.[78] As a result of this operating environment, RIRA members rely on active and passive support from local residents to hide from police and military authorities. Similarly, throughout the 1990s, Hamas relied on active and passive support from residents of the West Bank and Gaza Strip to hide its members from Israeli and Palestinian security forces.[79] Therefore,

---

[77]"Osama Bin Laden v. the U.S.: Edicts and Statements," *Frontline* [PBS Online], 2001, http://www.pbs.org/wgbh/pages/frontline/shows/binladen/who/edicts.html.

[78]Boyne (1998); Cowan (2002).

[79]Mishal and Sela (2000, pp. 157–163).

this operational space—provided by local support communities—allows the RIRA and Hamas members the ability to plan, train, and conduct terrorist attacks.

In contrast to RIRA and Hamas, FARC and al Qaeda both maintain a substantial degree of control over territory: FARC controls territory about the size of Switzerland in southern Colombia, and al Qaeda apparently maintains some control in the border regions between Afghanistan and Pakistan.[80] This sanctuary, although obviously not a requirement for all terrorist groups, provides these groups with a wide range of opportunities to expand their operations by planning more-sophisticated attacks, stockpiling weapons, and protecting their primary leaders. Indeed, FARC was able to use its control over the DMZ between 1998 and 2002 to develop its urban warfare capabilities and bolster its weapons supplies.[81] And, although the DMZ no longer exists, FARC still manages to sustain a degree of control over the area and its operational capabilities. Similarly, al Qaeda has demonstrated the importance it places on maintaining control over a sanctuary when, for example, in 2000 it explored Indonesia as a potential refuge.

Thus, as with the weapon requirement, we conclude that operational space is not sufficient in and of itself to explain terrorist groups' need for a safe haven to plan, train, and conduct operations. Terrorist groups with either a large cadre of fighters or the desire to plan sophisticated attacks appear to need more than just space, at least in the long term. Refugee camps, university campuses, and prisons, for example, serve as sufficient locations for sustaining a campaign, at least in the short term, or for planning relatively low-level attacks, but they cannot aid in sustaining the long-term expansion of group activities. Having said this, sanctuary clearly does not have to be state sponsored. Terrorist groups, such as FARC, can wrestle control from states or operate just as easily from the various "zones of chaos" scattered around the world.

---

[80]"U.S. Military Searching Afghan Mountains for Surviving Militants," *Washington Post*, January 29, 2003; Jawad Naeem, "Pakistan Joins War Against Al-Qaeda in Its Tribal Areas," *Christian Science Monitor*, June 28, 2002.

[81]"Los Planes de las Farc" (2000, p. 35).

Operational Security

In addition to operational space, we hypothesized that the four terrorist groups incorporated into this analysis would also work to maintain operational security. As such, this security is distinct from command and control *or* operational space because it incorporates the ability of terrorist groups to keep security forces from discovering the plans and people involved in a particular attack.[82] We would, therefore, expect that terrorists expend considerable resources to protect the integrity of their operations.

The RIRA uses its cell-like structure to maintain operational security, with individual members associated with local cells that operate relatively independently.[83] As a result, those in individual cells are not always aware of others' plans, reducing the potential for informers or infiltrators to disrupt any given attack. Although this structure has proven to be useful, an attack against one or more of the cells can halt the momentum of a group's terrorist campaign. Hamas currently faces this problem with regard to the intensive crackdown by Israeli authorities on bombmakers and midlevel leaders since 2000. In response, Hamas leaders have reportedly designated multiple teams for each operation: If Israeli authorities kill or arrest members of "Team A," another cell steps in and takes over without any instructions from higher command levels (which could potentially be discovered in transmission).[84] Therefore, this structure allows two cells to know the plans for a particular operation, making it more vulnerable to informants and infiltrators, but it also allows Hamas as a group to continue its attacks at a more consistent rate.

In comparison, FARC, a larger organization, must maintain its operational security over a wider geographic range. Multiple "fronts" in FARC serve the different operational roles: arms acquisitions, kidnapping, drug trafficking, guerrilla campaigns against military tar-

---

[82]For further discussion on the operational security requirements for terrorist groups, see Andrew R. Molnar, *Human Factors Considerations of Undergrounds in Insurgencies*, Hawaii: Special Operations Research Office of the American University, University of the Pacific Press, 1972 (reprinted 2001), pp. 101–108, 169–175.

[83]Dingley (2001, pp. 451–465).

[84]McGeary (2001, p. 52).

gets, and urban warfare.[85] Each front has its own operational security requirements; moreover, the group's central command must also coordinate these activities allowing the least amount of infiltration possible. FARC attempts to maintain operational security by holding meetings in areas of its control and uses trusted couriers, communication via cell phones, and radio transmitting stations (as mentioned previously). Yet Colombia's security forces have interrupted these meetings time and again, arresting key leaders, such as Josue Eliseo Prieto, FARC's chief financial officer, in July 1999.[86] Thus, security appears to be a significant point of vulnerability for this group.

Finally, an al Qaeda training manual found in the United Kingdom illustrates the value that the organization's leaders place on operational security: It includes advice on how to establish safe houses, maintain covers, and behave under interrogation.[87] Our case studies indicate, therefore, that operational security requirements expand as groups enlarge their activities. Yet, the relative degree and pattern of secrecy and isolation appear to remain the same despite the size of the terrorist organization.

Training

In addition to weapons and reliable weapon sources, we expect that most terrorist groups also need to provide their members with the technical skills to conduct attacks successfully. These skills could include bombmaking, weapon handling, and even operational security techniques.

Neither the RIRA nor Hamas actually controls large expanses of people and territory. As a result, time and space serve to constrain the groups' training opportunities. The RIRA has been able to avoid any difficulties that these constraints present by relying on the skills of previous PIRA members. Yet the same constraints have forced Hamas to use safe houses, refugee camps, university apartments,

---

[85]For examples, see "Armas por Coca" (1999).

[86]"General Tapias on Puerto Lleras Attack," *Semana,* July 11, 1999.

[87]U.S. Department of Justice, *Al Qaeda Training Manual,* excerpts found at www. usdoj.gov/ag/trainingmanual.htm (updated October 2002; accessed September 2003).

and sometimes even prisons as training grounds or as underground laboratories for future terrorist activities.[88] In an effort to expand their operational skills, Hamas members have also trained in Hizballah camps in southern Lebanon.[89] These camps have been a meeting place for Palestinians and Lebanese guerrillas since the late 1970s. Originally, Palestinians helped train local Lebanese militias; now, ironically, Hizballah, an offshoot of these militias, provides training to Palestinian terrorists.[90] Yet despite Hamas's desire to increase its capabilities, training activities risk exposure, and therefore the group must balance strengthening its capabilities with reducing operational security.[91]

Training is easier for FARC because of the group's control over people and territory in Colombia's southwestern departments, but it is much more essential. Because FARC's insurgent strategy necessitates that it directly challenge the Colombian security forces, the group therefore needs to train its members in guerrilla warfare tactics. While FARC has proven to be fairly skilled at ambushing government forces in the mountains, it historically has not been as successful in urban environments or its attempts at a terrorist campaign.[92] However, reports indicate that FARC has invited former IRA members to Colombia to help improve its urban operations capabilities.[93] If these reports are true, they suggest that even fairly capable terrorist groups

---

[88]U.S. Department of Justice, *Al Qaeda Training Manual*; Mishal and Sela (2000, pp. 75–81).

[89]Mishal and Sela (2000, pp. 64–65).

[90]For more information on the history of the militias and Hizballah, see Hala Jaber, *Hezbollah: Born with a Vengeance*, New York: Columbia University Press, 1997, pp. 15–21.

[91]Molnar (1972). See also Andrew R. Molnar, *Undergrounds in Insurgent, Revolutionary, and Resistance Warfare*, Washington, D.C.: American University, 1963, pp. 73–86.

[92]Despite a significant presence in Colombia's cities, such as Bogotá, FARC has not been as successful in its urban campaign as in its guerrilla attacks. For example, despite repeated attempts, FARC was not able to assassinate now-President Alvaro Uribe during his presidential campaign in 2002. Yet this pattern changed after the alleged training from former IRA cadres, as the group conducted more and more successful urban attacks in early 2003. For more information, see "Colombia Blasts Kill 13 as Uribe Takes Office," *CNN.com*, August 8, 2002.

[93]For more information, see Henry McDonald, "IRA Manuals Discovered in Colombia," *Guardian Unlimited*, December 16, 2001.

might go outside their own organization to develop new technical skills.

A number of examples demonstrate the importance that al Qaeda places on training. First, its *Declaration of Jihad* includes a discussions on training new operatives, communicating safely, blending in with a foreign society, and choosing training locations, instructors, and trainees.[94] Second, not only have al Qaeda's leaders written on the importance of training, but they also adhered to these instructions in preparing for the September 11, 2001, attacks; members of the Hamburg cell apparently received training in or near Afghanistan before traveling to the United States to enroll in flight schools.[95] Al Qaeda's camps in Afghanistan also provided training opportunities to other Arab and Southeast Asian fighters.[96] This allowed al Qaeda not only to train and develop the capabilities of future "affiliates" but also to solidify its relationship with like-minded groups.

Training therefore appears to be multipurposed: first, terrorist groups provide their members with a basic level of technical skills; second, terrorist organizations reach out to other groups to supplement their own capabilities; and third, terrorists use training activities to establish relationships with other like-minded groups, possibly as an investment for future cooperation or help. For the first and primary requirement, this degree of training follows a similar pattern throughout our four case studies. Yet the degree and type of "supplemental" or expertise training appears to vary according to the needs and objectives of the terrorist organization. Similarly the "relationship" role of training is, at this point, an innovative al Qaeda approach.

Intelligence

For the purpose of this report, we define *intelligence* as the basic information that terrorists need to identify a potential target, plan a

---

[94]*Declaration of Jihad Against the Country's Tyrants* (trans.).

[95]For more information on the Hamburg cell, see "Man Alleged to Aid 9/11 Cell Arrested in German Inquiry" (2002), and "German at Center of Sept. 11 Inquiry: Suspect Recruited Hijackers in Hamburg," *Washington Post*, June 12, 2002.

[96]Anonymous (2002, pp. 153–193).

method of attack, and correctly understand the response that such an attack will garner from their intended audience. Logically, we expect that the degree to which terrorist groups need intelligence will be directly related to the sophistication of the planned attack. For example, in 1997, al-Gama'at al-Islamiyya (IG) gunned down and killed 58 foreigners and four Egyptians exiting a tourist bus at Hapshetsut's Temple in Luxor, Egypt.[97] To conduct this attack, the IG's "intelligence" had to indicate that foreigners would be at the temple (a fairly safe assumption, since it is a major tourist site) and that an attack would pressure the Egyptian government economically as foreign tourism decreased.[98] In the case of the IG attack, the intelligence used was fairly intuitive and did not need considerable reconnaissance or planning. In contrast, the September 11, 2001, attacks apparently took several years for al Qaeda to plan and eventually carry out and required considerable intelligence; moreover, the intelligence gathering had to be done in unfamiliar territory.[99] Despite this variety, we can expect that all four terrorist groups in our study exhibit a basic level of intelligence capabilities.

During its campaign against British authorities in Northern Ireland and England, PIRA members put significant effort into developing their reconnaissance and intelligence-gathering techniques.[100] Thus, we expect that the RIRA members would similarly demonstrate the ability to conduct surveillance and other intelligence activities. Yet at this point, none of the RIRA's activities has demonstrated the same degree of sophistication as the former PIRA attacks have. Intelligence requirements for the Omagh bomb were basically on par with the

---

[97]Ian O. Lessor, Bruce Hoffman, John Arquilla, David F. Ronfeldt, and Michele Zanini, *Countering the New Terrorism*, Santa Monica, Calif.: RAND Corporation, MR-989-AF, 1999, p. 60.

[98]Jon B. Alterman, "The Luxor Shootout and Egypt's Armed Islamist Opposition," *Policywatch*, No. 279, November 17, 1997.

[99]Spanish authorities arrested a suspected al Qaeda member and found "surveillance" tapes of U.S. landmarks, including the World Trade Center, the Brooklyn Bridge, the Statue of Liberty, a New York airport, the Sears Tower, the Golden Gate Bridge, Disneyland, and Universal Studios. The tapes were allegedly shot by Ghasoub Abrash Ghalyoun in 1997. See Walter Pincus, "Spain Says Al-Qaeda Suspect Videotaped Towers, Other Landmarks," *Washington Post*, July 17, 2002, p. A17.

[100]For more information, see J. Bowyer Bell, *IRA Tactics and Targets: An Analysis of Tactical Aspects of the Armed Struggle 1969–1989*, New Brunswick, N.J.: Transaction Publishers, 1991.

Luxor attack described above. Therefore, it appears that—at its current capability level ("1" on the framework in Chapter Two)—the RIRA does not have the need for intelligence capabilities beyond a basic understanding of its local operating environment.

Similarly, Hamas's activities, until recently, only demonstrated the need for a basic level of intelligence and included bus schedules, security procedures at a particular café, and ways to enter Israel from the West Bank or Gaza undetected. Yet, as the activities of Hamas have expanded since the advent of the al-Aqsa intifada, so have its intelligence requirements. For example, in July 2002, Hamas detonated a bomb inside the cafeteria most frequented by international students at the Hebrew University of Jerusalem.[101] The university is and had been surrounded by walls and fences, with security posts at all its entrances, and security guards check students' identification cards and bags before they are admitted onto the campus. To gain access to this university cafeteria, therefore, Hamas needed intelligence on the school's security arrangements and protocols. Israeli authorities believe that Hamas specifically targeted a cafeteria with international students, requiring Hamas members to know which one of the campuses many cafeterias was the most frequented by foreign students.[102] News sources have subsequently reported that Hamas was able to obtain its information from Mohammed Oudeh, a worker on campus who was recruited specifically for the attack.[103] Israeli security forces arrested Oudeh in August 2002.

FARC also has a fairly developed intelligence network in and around Colombia. Although it is difficult to determine whether this network revolves around the group's activities in the drug trade, guerrilla warfare, terrorism, or a combination of all three, recent events have evidenced that FARC pays special attention to intelligence. For example, in August 2000, members of a Colombian military brigade assassinated a fellow soldier because they suspected him of collabo-

---

[101]Israeli authorities believed a 15-person cell of Hamas conducted this attack. This same cell was responsible for an attack on a Jerusalem café in March 2002. For more information, see "Five Hamas Members Nabbed for Hebrew University Bombing," Associated Press, August 22, 2002.

[102]"Five Hamas Members Nabbed for Hebrew University Bombing"(2002).

[103]"Jerusalem Blasts Kills 7; 4 Americans Among Dead," *CNN.com*, August 1, 2002.

rating with FARC.[104] Such events indicate that FARC uses at least some of its drug-trafficking revenue to maintain a network of informants in Colombia's security forces. Similarly, FARC has also demonstrated that it studies Colombia's counterinsurgency tactics and employs reconnaissance teams into areas before it attacks. For example, the group frequently investigates the terrain surrounding a particular village that it plans to target in order to draw out Colombia's military forces; FARC forces then hide and lay booby traps along the most logical access route for the government soldiers responding to such an attack.[105] Through such methods, FARC claimed a series of victories over the battered Colombian forces between 1998 and 2000. Initially, Black Hawk helicopters that the U.S. government provided to Colombia as part of Plan Colombia in 2000 allowed security forces to flank these hidden booby traps and defeat FARC in these skirmishes. But soon after, FARC began choosing its fights more carefully, picking mountainous terrain that provided only one place for a helicopter to land; this reconnaissance once again allowed rebel fighters to wait for the arriving helicopter and shoot soldiers as they exited the aircraft.[106] These examples demonstrate that intelligence and reconnaissance activities are key to the success of FARC's campaign.

Even more so than FARC, the amount of time that al Qaeda's members spend to prepare for their group's "spectacular attacks" appears to be the result of meticulous intelligence gathering, in addition to the training and operational security requirements discussed above. Reconnaissance tapes discovered in Spain in July 2002 show how al Qaeda sent out advance teams to scout potential targets four years before the September 11 attacks on the World Trade Center and the Pentagon.[107] Al Qaeda's preparation for the bombing of the USS *Cole* demonstrated similar levels of reconnaissance, with a team sent to survey, plan, and prepare for the attack with help from local dissi-

---

[104]"El Silencio de las Armas," *Cambio*, August, 14, 2000.

[105]These tactics were a point of discussion at a conference held by the Center for Naval Analyses in October 2000 and attended by the author (Cragin). See also "La Batalla de Córdoba," *Cambio*, May 24, 1999, p. 32.

[106]"La Batalla de Córdoba" (1999).

[107]For more on al Qaeda's planning, see Bergen (2001, especially pp. 109–110). See Walter Pincus (2002, p. A17).

dents.[108] Moreover, al Qaeda has gone beyond using simple intelli-gence-gathering and reconnaissance activities; its members engage in counterintelligence activities, attempting to confuse and deceive state authorities. For example, the "Islamic Army for the Liberation of the Holy Places" claimed the 1998 attacks on U.S. embassies in Kenya and Tanzania.[109] Although we now attribute these attacks to al Qaeda, the misdirection was enough to cause authorities some con-fusion at the time.[110]

The four terrorist groups in this analysis all require basic intelli-gence-gathering skills to successfully conduct their attacks, including an accurate understanding of their local operating environment and the effect of an attack on their adversaries. Yet it appears that terror-ist groups operating at sophisticated levels—in this instance, al Qaeda is ranked "5" on our capability metric—also require deception skills to sustain a high degree of terrorist capability.

Money

Finally, we would expect that all terrorist groups need financial resources to conduct a series of successful attacks.[111] As such, money is best considered an operational tool, rather than a tool that pro-motes group cohesion over the long term. The following section, therefore, examines the extent to which terrorist groups operating at various capability levels—as exemplified by the four organizations analyzed—require money to sustain their terrorist campaigns.

Because the RIRA is a small organization and its financial needs are relatively minor, it is difficult to identify the extent to which *money* affects its operational capabilities. It is clear, however, that the RIRA does not pay most of its members a salary. Many in the group con-tinue to work to support themselves and their families. Similarly,

---

[108]International Crisis Group, "Yemen: Coping with Terrorism and Violence in a Frag-ile State," January 8, 2003.

[109]Judy Aita, "U.S. Completes Presentation of Evidence in Embassy Bombing Trial," U.S. Department of State, Office of International Information Programs, n.d. (accessed September 2003).

[110]Aita (n.d.).

[111]For further discussion, see Molnar (1963, p. 61) and Bell (1990, pp. 193–211).

some reports suggest that the group is trying to reengage old PIRA fundraising networks through such means as diaspora support, theft, and credit card fraud. Yet the amount of money the RIRA has been able to draw from these networks seems to be relatively minor.[112] We conclude, therefore, that groups that operate at relatively low capability levels do not require significant resources to sustain their terrorist operations.

In comparison, Hamas appears to place more emphasis on securing resources. For example, Hamas solicits funds from Palestinian diaspora communities located within the United States.[113] Notably, Hamas does not use these resources solely for its terrorist operations; for example, it sponsors a number of charities in the West Bank and Gaza Strip. Thus, when Western media report that Hamas is receiving funds from such countries as Saudi Arabia and Iran, it is difficult to separate the funds the organization uses to support health clinics from those used to purchase explosives on the black market.[114] Therefore, although money is key for Hamas to sustain its activities, it also plays an organizational role—group cohesion—by bolstering its relationship to local communities and further legitimizing its activities in the Arab world.

In some ways, FARC follows the pattern of the RIRA and Hamas, but in other ways its experience is clearly distinct from either group with regard to money. For example, FARC maintains a professional cadre, whose members receive a salary in addition to uniforms, radios, weapons, and ammunition supplies.[115] Thus, FARC is able to bolster group cohesion by providing its members with financial incentives to join and stay with the group. This parallels Hamas's support for charitable organizations in the West Bank and Gaza Strip, which

---

[112]For more information, see Dingley (2001, pp. 451–465) and "Corkman in Charge as Real IRA Threat Remains" (2001).

[113]For more information, see Steven Emerson, *American Jihad: The Terrorists Living Among Us,* New York: The Free Press, 2002, pp. 79–108.

[114]For examples of such reports, see Yohanan Ramati, "Islamic Fundamentalism Gaining," *Midstream,* Vol. 39, No. 2, 1993, p. 2, and Steven Emerson, "Meltdown," *The New Republic,* November 23, 1992, p. 27.

[115]For more information on the finances of FARC, see "Los Costos del Cese al Fuego," *El País,* July 6, 2000; "El Otro Plan Colombia," *Cambio,* March 20, 2000, pp. 25–26; and "Farc se Movilizan al Sur de Bolívar," *El Tiempo,* July 16, 2000.

often funnel food and shelter to its members and their families. Yet, FARC has higher requirements for training, weapon supplies, operational security, and intelligence, all of which necessitate a constant outpouring of funds. FARC's involvement in the drug economy is therefore an essential component of its ability to sustain both a high level of operational capabilities and group cohesion over the medium and long term.

Finally, al Qaeda's operations demonstrate the group's significant need for financial resources. Its members appear to travel frequently—for training, planning meetings, or to conduct specific attacks—and often require false travel documents to do so.[116] Similarly, al Qaeda's bases discovered in Afghanistan revealed communications equipment and computers, as well as research sites for the development of chemical and biological weapons.[117] In addition, Osama bin Laden funneled significant resources into countries in which he stayed, such as Sudan, building businesses and sponsoring infrastructure development.[118] Al Qaeda has also "sponsored" other like-minded terrorist groups, such as the GSPC and the ASG. Thus, the cases of both FARC and al Qaeda demonstrate that as a terrorist group expands the sophistication of its attacks as well as its reach, it requires a parallel expansion of funds. Furthermore, these funds can be used both to sustain the terrorist group's operational capabilities and help fulfill its organizational requirements.

Money does not adequately describe terrorist groups' true operational needs nor is it exclusively an operational requirement. Indeed, all four of the cases indicate that, for terrorist groups, money can act as an adhesive to maintain group cohesion. As such, this "cohesion" requirement might be defined better as *food and shelter for terrorists and their families.* Moreover, for terrorist groups operating at high capability levels, such as FARC and al Qaeda, the key operational

---

[116]Michael Buchanan, "Europe's Hunt for Al-Qaeda," *BBC News* [online], September 6, 2002.

[117]Shelia MacVicar and Henry Schuster, "European Terror Suspects Got Al Qaeda Training, Sources Say," *CNN.com*, February 6, 2003; Nick Farrell, "US Fears Nuclear Cyber Terror Attacks," *vnunet.com*, June 27, 2002.

[118]Sharon Theimer, "Like Terror Network, Bin Laden's Money Trail Reaches Around the Globe," Associated Press, September 19, 2001.

requirement does not appear to be large amounts of money provided in a lump sum, but rather a steady stream of income.

Observations on Operational Tools

We draw three primary observations from this analysis. First, of the seven tools that we initially hypothesized as terrorist groups' operational requirements, three appear to be the most consistent across our case studies: command and control networks, weapons, and operational security. Admittedly, this analysis only provides a first look at terrorist groups' operational needs; much more could be done. Yet the four case studies do represent a wide variety of capability levels, objectives, and operating environments, so this consistency is, arguably, noteworthy; however, it does not *necessarily* equate to terrorists' greatest vulnerabilities. Terrorists seem to have the ability to improvise in their attacks or locate *weapons* on the black market, making themselves a difficult target for counterterrorism policy. Yet this consistency does imply that surveillance activities at and around U.S. borders or overseas could affect the full range of terrorist threats, making it one of the more efficient counterterrorism tactics. Similarly, attacks on command and control networks should effectively reduce the operational capabilities of all terrorist groups, regardless of their size, objectives, operating environment, or sophistication.

This analysis also revealed an important dynamic between the requirements of leadership and command and control networks. One of the primary findings in the previous section was that terrorist groups with multiple layers and a cadre of midlevel leaders are not as vulnerable to attacks on their leadership. But these groups are vulnerable to attacks on their command and control networks. Thus, a counterterrorism strategy that *coordinates* attacks on terrorist leaders and command and control networks may serve not only to disrupt the operational ability of multilayered groups but also to demoralize midlevel cadres—enough that it negatively affects group cohesion.

Second, the following four of our initial seven organizational requirements exhibited a significant amount of variety across the case studies: operational space, training, intelligence, and money.

We are not convinced that this variety is attributable solely to differences in group objectives, modus operandi, and operating environments. Indeed, all four terrorist groups included in this analysis required *some degree* of operational space, training, intelligence, and money. However, in the case of money, we determined that, for many groups, it performs an organizational role by sustaining group cohesion. Thus, money becomes a significant operational requirement only once a group needs a steady influx of funds to pay members, prepare for attacks years in advance, and conduct sophisticated reconnaissance and counterintelligence campaigns. Similarly, all the terrorist groups use a basic form of intelligence gathering for their attacks, and groups like al Qaeda practice deception techniques as well. In fact, these four requirements can arguably be divided further into seven, including the following additional three: sanctuary separated from operational space, technical expertise and specialists from training, and deception from intelligence. The policy implication of this observation is that it shifts the counterterrorism focus from *commonalities* to the *incremental differences* between terrorist groups operating at various capability levels. Thus, we adjusted our list of operational requirements, adding four additional resources as follows: command and control, weapons, operational space, operational security, training, basic intelligence, technical expertise and specialists, external weapon sources, sanctuary, money, and deception skills.

Finally, we conclude that each of the last five requirements listed above—technical expertise, external weapons sources, sanctuary, money, and deception skills—serve as indicators that a terrorist group has attempted to increase its operational capabilities. For example, if a group begins to augment its training activities, or seeks help from mercenaries or other terrorist groups to develop its technical expertise, U.S. policymakers should consider means to disrupt the training, especially if the terrorists have demonstrated anti-U.S. sentiment. Similarly, U.S. counterterrorism policy that targets a particular terrorist group's access to external weapons has the potential to degrade its ability to conduct more-sophisticated campaigns. The same could be true of U.S. policies that attempt to eliminate potential "zones of chaos" or safe havens available to terrorist organizations and counterintelligence activities that work to penetrate terrorists' deception tactics.

The purpose of this analysis is to inform U.S. counterterrorism policymakers by outlining what terrorist groups need to function—organizationally and operationally—and to recommend ways the U.S. government can use counterterrorism resources more effectively. To do this, the report has focused, thus far, on terrorist groups as static entities. This approach poses some difficulties for the policymaker because, as we discussed in the previous chapter, terrorist groups often adapt and change to their environmental surroundings. The next chapter therefore takes our analysis one step further and attempts to examine how terrorist groups evolve according to their internal group dynamics, as well as how they respond to external stimuli.

Chapter Four

TERRORIST GROUPS AS DYNAMIC ENTITIES

Terrorist groups do not stand still. They grow and sometimes fade, responding to changes in their political, social, economic, and security environments. The previous two chapters presented a framework for assessing the relative threats, capabilities, and requirements of terrorist groups in the context of the struggle against terrorism. Yet these chapters do not address how terrorists might evolve within the framework. To address this issue, we discuss in this chapter some of the terrorist groups that have shown significant changes over time—and what appears to have caused these shifts. We do not propose a new model, in addition to the framework outlined in Chapters Two and Three, but instead we simply attempt to refine the picture of terrorist threats to the United States and U.S. interests overseas by adding a dynamic element to our framework.

To do this, we assess the evolution of four terrorist groups: Peru's Shining Path, Lebanese Hizballah, Egyptian Islamic Jihad, and the Philippine Abu Sayyaf Group. We chose these four groups because they have evolved in dissimilar circumstances, articulate diverse objectives, and some even have different organizational structures. As such, they illustrate a wide range of potential changes. We examine the evolutionary trajectories of these four groups in the context of our framework, concluding with a discussion of the potential implications that the dynamic nature of terrorism has for U.S. counterterrorism policy.

SHINING PATH

The Shining Path, or SL, began in the 1960s under the leadership of Abiemael Guzmán Reynoso in Ayacucho, a rural district in southeastern Peru.[1] The SL's initial strategy, when it first emerged as a Marxist organization, was to establish a peasant base in Peru's rural communities.[2] The terrorist group continued to expand through the 1980s, and by 1990 the SL was threatening Peru's urban centers.[3] Yet in 1992, the Shining Path collapsed. This section highlights the key factors that, in our assessment, both enabled SL's expansion and influenced this collapse.

The SL conducted its first official terrorist attack in 1980, opposing Peru's new democratically elected government.[4] Following this attack, the SL continued to expand its activities but focused most of its resources in Peru's rural southeast. Indeed, the Peruvian government's general lack of presence in Ayacucho and the area's somewhat isolated culture allowed the SL to solidify its support bases in the early 1980s.[5] This expansion culminated in a series of terrorist attacks on transmission towers, located throughout Peru's mountainous regions, which provide electricity to Lima.[6] In response to these attacks, Peru's security authorities instigated counterattacks on the SL and its support communities. Such policies included the creation of a military-controlled zone, widespread civilian arrests, and attacks on known and suspected SL members.[7] This counterinsurgency campaign proved successful in the short term, disrupting the group's command and control as well as its operational capabilities.

---

[1]For a discussion of the development and evolution of the SL, see Gustavo Gorriti, *The Shining Path: A History of the Millenarian War in Peru* (Robin Kirk, trans.), Chapel Hill, N.C.: University of North Carolina Press, 1999.

[2]Gorriti (1999).

[3]David Scott Palmer, ed., *The Shining Path of Peru*, 2nd edition, New York: St. Martin's Press, 1994, p. 34.

[4]For a discussion on the progression of the SL's terrorist activities, see Gorriti (1999), pp. 67–88.

[5]Gorriti (1999).

[6]David Scott Palmer, "The Revolutionary Terrorism of Peru's Shining Path," in Martha Crenshaw, ed., *Terrorism in Context*, State College, Pa.: Pennsylvania State University Press, 1995, pp. 294–295.

[7]Palmer (1995).

Conversely, it also appeared to contribute to an increase in popular support for the SL, allowing the organization to begin recruitment in Peru's cities in addition to the rural southeast.[8]

Despite its initial losses, the SL was able to reconstitute after the series of counterattacks by Peru's security authorities. By 1985, the SL was steadily increasing the number of attacks on Peru's urban centers.[9] This increase appeared to be a conscious effort on the part of the SL leadership to challenge the Peruvian government.[10] The SL was able to accomplish this escalation, in part, as a result of its control over the Upper Huallaga Valley. This area produced a substantial portion of the Peruvian coca crops in the 1980s and, therefore, provided the SL with access to funds from the drug economy. In fact, the SL was able to win enough popular support in this area that it convinced residents to fight against government security forces on behalf of the group.[11] Moreover, the taxes that the SL drew from the production of narcotics allowed it to expand its weapons, training, and infrastructure in support of its urban strategy.[12]

By the time Peruvians elected Alberto Fujimori as president in 1990, the country was in the midst of political and economic chaos.[13] A significant portion of this chaos was attributed to the SL: More than 23,000 people died from terrorist attacks in Peru from May 1982 to September 1992.[14] Moreover, by 1992 the SL was beginning to threaten Lima itself. In response to this threat, Fujimori suspended the courts and congress and declared emergency rule to fight cor-

---

[8]Palmer (1995); Kees Koonings and Dirk Kruijt, eds., *Societies of Fear: The Legacy of Civil War, Violence and Terror in Latin America*, London: Zed Books, 1999, p. 43.

[9]For a discussion of the SL urban campaigns, see Gordon McCormick, *From the Sierra to the Cities: The Urban Campaign of the Shining Path*, Santa Monica, Calif.: RAND Corporation, R-4150-USDP, 1992.

[10]McCormick (1992).

[11]McCormick (1992).

[12]For a discussion of the SL's expansion into the Upper Huallaga Valley, see Cynthia McClintock, *Revolutionary Movements in Latin America: El Salvador's FMLN and Peru's Shining Path*, Washington, D.C.: U.S. Institute of Peace Press, 1998, pp. 86–89, 271–280.

[13]Carlos Basombrío, "Peace in Peru: An Unfinished Task," in Arnson (1999, pp. 206–208).

[14]Palmer (1994, p. 34).

ruption and the SL.[15] He also designated a counterterrorism strategy that specifically targeted the SL leadership. This contrasted with prior strategies that focused on operations against SL supporters in the rural communities.[16]

To target the SL leadership, however, authorities needed better intelligence.[17] The government therefore began to gather information from captured SL members, using special legislative powers that allowed them to detain potential terrorists without a trial.[18] To illustrate the momentum gained by these techniques, the number of SL members killed after capture (without a trial) doubled between 1989 and 1992.[19] In addition to these intensified counterterrorism efforts, the very nature of the SL's activities allowed for easier access to intelligence. As the SL moved into the cities, the Peruvian authorities were able to penetrate the organization more easily and gather information on the leadership's whereabouts.[20] Finally, in September 1992, authorities arrested SL leader Abiemael Guzmán and captured the archives of the SL's central command. Police and military authorities eventually arrested twelve members of the SL leadership and killed an additional five, which had represented 60 percent of the total central command.[21]

The SL could not recover from the loss of Guzmán. The structure of the SL group was such that the central command made broad strategy choices, and, once it was removed, the group was without national leadership.[22] Although regional leaders had been responsible for operational planning, they were unable to successfully fill the national leadership vacuum. Guzmán also represented more than

---

[15]Palmer (1994).

[16]Koonings and Kruijt (1999, p. 43).

[17]Arnson (1999, p. 231).

[18]"Glimmering Path," *The Economist*, July 29, 1995; Palmer (1994, p. 18).

[19]Arnson (1999, p. 229).

[20]James Brooke, "Snaring the Top Guerrilla: 'Bingo! We Got Him,'" *New York Times*, September 15, 1992.

[21]Russell Watson and Brook Larmer, "It's Your Turn to Lose," *Newsweek*, September 28, 1992.

[22]Gordon H. McCormick, *The Shining Path and the Future of Peru*, Santa Monica, Calif.: RAND Corporation, R-3781-DOS/OSD, 1990.

just a strategist; he had cultivated and maintained control over the moral strength of the group from the beginning.[23] Moreover, most of his original second-tier leaders had been killed in the 1980s, and there was not a succession plan.[24] Therefore, after Guzmán's arrest, the SL crumbled from within the core of the organization. It eventually dissolved into multiple small groups, which have not yet regained the organizational structure and unity of the original 5,000-strong Shining Path.[25]

Other factors also influenced the decimation of the SL. To sustain its urban campaign, the SL leadership increased the taxes on its local support base in the late 1980s. Failure to pay these "taxes" resulted in attacks on rural communities, the SL's traditional support base.[26] In response, some peasant communities withdrew their support for the SL and allied themselves with the Peruvian military, forming civil defense groups to counter the SL.[27] Rural support for SL decreased significantly, and communities that had once fought with SL guerrillas against the government switched sides, allying themselves with the military. This decline in rural support, combined with improved government counterterrorism tactics, reduced the SL's ability to train and operate even in its primary support bases.[28]

Finally, President Fujimori not only instituted an aggressive counterterrorism campaign but also successfully managed Guzmán's arrest. A key factor in the collapse of the Shining Path was the disillusionment of Guzmán's followers. President Fujimori solidified this disillusionment by allowing Guzmán to make a public statement upon his arrest—at which time he urged SL members to continue to fight—and then publishing a contradictory letter from Guzmán that told the

---

[23]McCormick (1990).

[24]Watson and Larmer (1992).

[25]Oscar Ramirez, the man responsible for a series of attack on hotels in 1995, is thought to be the leader of the strongest of these small groups.

[26]Gabriela Tarazona-Sevillano, "The Organization of the Shining Path," in Palmer (1994, p. 204).

[27]Tarazona-Sevillano (1994); Cynthia McClintock, "The Decimation of Peru's Sendero Luminoso," in Arnson (1999, pp. 235–237).

[28]Tarazona-Sevillano (1994). See also Brooke (1992) for a discussion of Peru's intelligence capabilities in urban areas versus rural areas.

SL to lay down its arms.[29] By 1992, the Shining Path had lost its leader, its support base, and its members were disillusioned.

Observations

This brief look at SL's history provides insight into the potential evolutionary trajectories of terrorist groups, especially in the context of our framework. First, the SL's ability to conduct terrorist attacks developed fairly linearly, along our capabilities thresholds: Over a period of approximately 10 years, the SL progressed from having the ability to conduct *any* terrorist attack to possessing the capacity to successfully attack guarded targets. Furthermore, this progression appears to have mirrored the SL's strategic requirements as it moved from a rural to urban insurgency. This first observation has significant implications for our analytical framework. It reveals that the SL's decisionmaking, at this point, was based primarily on how best to achieve the organization's strategic objectives. External factors, such as state sponsorship, did not have a noteworthy impact on its expansion. The group's ability to pursue its strategic objectives resulted, in part, from its access to necessary resources through the drug economy. But other key factors that enabled this expansion also played a role, including easy access to recruitment pools as well as operational space.

Second, in contrast to its expansion, the Shining Path *deteriorated* rapidly. Over a period of two years, the group's capabilities diminished from having the ability to attack guarded targets successfully to not even being able to conduct any type of attack. Admittedly, a combination of factors contributed to this deterioration. Yet it is clear from the above discussion that Fujimori's counterterrorism strategy was a key factor, as it reduced the effectiveness of the SL's command and control structure. Indeed, security forces were able to remove more than half of the SL leadership. Without a secure com-

---

[29]Corinne Schmidt, "Guzmán Fights on from the Cage," *The Times* [London], September 26, 1992; Sally Bowen, "Peru Rebel Chief 'Seeks Peace Deal,'" *Financial Times*, October 2, 1993. In his first address, President Fujimori allowed Guzmán to appear before the press and make a speech. Reporters claimed that Fujimori was attempting to minimize the legend of Guzmán by dressing him in prison clothes and keeping him in a cage. For Guzmán's later statement, Fujimori presented a letter to the press, supposedly from Guzmán, offering a peace agreement.

mand and control infrastructure, the group was forced to expend resources on hiding and surviving, rather than conducting its urban campaign. Overreaching and unprepared to operate in cities, the group's command and control was vulnerable to external factors, or influences exogenous to the group, such as surveillance and counter-intelligence. Thus, although these external factors did not help to ex-pand the group's capabilities, they did play a role in the SL's deterio-ration.

Finally, the Shining Path's deterioration also resulted from the group's failure to sustain popular support. The organization's attacks and taxes against its own rural constituency—in an effort to sustain its urban campaigns—undermined its support base. Notably, the Peruvian government effectively exploited this weakness through the establishment of local self-defense forces in the rural southeast. Simi-larly, the Peruvian government was able to dishearten the militant organization's own members by delegitimizing Guzmán, as men-tioned above, by depicting their leader as a hypocrite. Therefore, internal group dynamics—specifically the relationships between the SL and its support base as well as between Guzmán and SL mem-bers—weakened the organization and contributed to its demise.

HIZBALLAH

Hizballah ("Party of God") presents a different, contrasting evolution to the Shining Path. In the 1970s and early 1980s, Palestinian terror-ists used southern Lebanon as a base for their attacks on northern Israel.[30] During this same period, the minority Shiite population of Lebanon was engaged in a struggle for national power with the country's Maronite Christians. Because the Maronites were also sometimes allies of Israel, the Palestinians helped train and equip Shiite militias in southern Lebanon to fight against the Christians.[31] These militias would eventually form Hizballah. Thus, Hizballah's roots were based in both the Palestinian-Israeli conflict and Lebanon's civil war. As a result, the group's strategic objectives were

---

[30]For more information on Israel's counterterrorism activities in southern Lebanon against Palestinian guerrillas, see Ian Black and Benny Morris, *Israel's Secret Wars: A History of Israel's Intelligence Services*, New York: Grove Weidenfeld, 1991.

[31]Jaber (1997, p. 17).

twofold: to remove the Israeli military presence from southern Lebanon, and to gain political power in Lebanon.[32] Notably, unlike the Shining Path, Hizballah has managed to achieve the first objective and has made progress toward the second in the past 20 years. The following section outlines the factors that have enabled and impeded Hizballah's success.

The primary event that sparked the development of Hizballah was Israel's invasion and occupation of southern Lebanon in 1982.[33] South Lebanon's Shiite community initially welcomed the invasion with some relief, as they were beginning to revile the PLO for its corruption and internecine violence.[34] Yet the Shiites eventually realized that the Israeli military did not plan on leaving southern Lebanon. Thus, the continued Israeli occupation led to the outbreak of sporadic and disorganized acts of resistance by local militias.[35]

In November 1982, Hizballah conducted its first large-scale terrorist attack, a suicide bombing of the Israeli military headquarters in Tyre, which killed 141 people.[36] A number of factors contributed to the scattered militia's ability to organize and develop its capabilities to conduct this attack. Arguably, the most significant component was the training provided to the Shiite militias by the more than 1,500 Iranian Revolutionary Guards sent to help in the resistance to Israel. The Revolutionary Guards organized the militias and trained them on conducting effective attacks; the training included reconnaissance, intelligence gathering, and suicide bombing tactics. The training camps established by the Revolutionary Guards also taught the militia members Iran's revolutionary doctrine.[37] As a result of its

---

[32]For a discussion of Hizballah's ideology, political objectives, and military strategy, see Amal Saad-Ghorayeb, *Hizbu'llah: Politics and Religion*, London: Pluto Press, 2002, chapters 1 and 6.

[33]Saad-Ghorayeb (2002, p. 10).

[34]Jaber (1997, pp. 14–18).

[35]For a chronology of these attacks, see the RAND Terrorism Chronology, accessible at http://db.mipt.org.

[36]RAND Terrorism Chronology (http://db.mipt.org).

[37]For information on the impact that the Iranian revolution had on the Shi'ite militias, see Saad-Ghorayeb (2002, pp. 14–15). See also "Baalbek Seen as Staging Area for Terrorism," *Washington Post*, January 9, 1984, and Carl Anthony Wege, "Hizbollah Organization," *Studies in Conflict and Terrorism*, Vol. 17, 1994, pp. 151–164.

new organizational structure and training, Hizballah was able to expand its abilities even further, conducting a suicide vehicle attack on the U.S. embassy in Beirut, which killed 63 people, in April 1983 and, six months later, bombing the U.S. Marine Corps barracks in Beirut, killing 241 people. Between 1982 and 1985, Hizballah conducted at least 30 suicide attacks, killing more than 400 people.[38]

In response to the threat posed by Hizballah's new and increasing capabilities, Israeli forces in the mid-1980s began to focus their activities on eliminating the organization's leaders.[39] In addition to this counterterrorism tactic, the Israeli military also began to attack the Lebanese Shiite population directly, believing that the people would blame Hizballah for these reprisals and reduce their support for the organization.[40] Initially, Israel's counterattacks worked, resulting in the loss of operational capabilities and public support for Hizballah.[41] However, Hizballah was able to survive this loss. A key enabling factor was the Hizballah's establishment of relief services, which were supported by the financial backing of Iran, to help the Shiite population recover and rebuild following the Israeli attacks.[42] Thus, even though the Shiite population continued to suffer Israeli reprisal attacks, Hizballah made it possible for them to recover quickly. This activity guaranteed Hizballah a strong base of support.

The group also responded to Israeli pressure by securing command and control structures and increasing its focus on internal security. For example, Hizballah leaders would conceive of a new operation but refrain from telling the rank and file until just prior to the execution of the operation.[43] The operatives carrying out the attacks were taught to dress in civilian clothing, shave their beards, and refrain

---

[38]For a chronology of these attacks, see the RAND Terrorism Chronology (http://db.mipt.org).

[39]Black and Morris (1991, pp. 394–399).

[40]Jaber (1997, pp. 156–157).

[41]Jaber (1997).

[42]Jaber (1997, pp. 167–168); Wege (1994, pp. 157–159); Saad-Ghorayeb (2002, pp. 7–33); Bruce W. Nelan, "What's Peace Got to Do with It?" *Time*, August 9, 1993, pp. 32–33.

[43]Jaber (1997, pp. 39–40).

from carrying weapons to avoid suspicion.[44] Similarly, the organization began to recruit and develop technical experts as well as concentrate more resources on intelligence-gathering and reconnaissance activities. These changes improved the group's operational security, increasing the success of Hizballah's attacks on Israeli military forces.

In addition, Hizballah restructured its organization, layering its leadership.[45] The reorganization ensured that Israeli counterattacks would not destroy the entire group. The success of this change was seen, for example, in February 1992, when Israeli military helicopters shot and killed Abbas al-Musawi, then leader of Hizballah, and his family in the southern Lebanese village of Jibshit.[46] Yet Hizballah was still able to sustain its campaign against Israel. After al-Musawi's assassination, Hizballah experienced an internal leadership struggle, from which the current leader, Hassan Nasrallah, emerged.[47] Although this struggle revealed some weaknesses, it indicated that, unlike the Shining Path, Hizballah could survive the loss of key leaders.

In May 2000, Israeli forces withdrew from southern Lebanon. This withdrawal is viewed widely as a triumph for Hizballah by other terrorist groups in the region, particularly Palestinians, as well as proof that a terrorist campaign can succeed. Hizballah's victory stands in stark contrast to the failure of the Shining Path's campaign, especially given the parallels between Peru and Israel's counterterrorism strategies. Yet Hizballah did not successfully make the shift from a rural to urban insurgency. In fact, Hizballah did not need an urban campaign to achieve its objectives because its objective was to remove Israel from southern Lebanon, not take control of people and territory within the Israeli state. As a result, Hizballah did not need to stretch either its resources or infrastructure and potentially expose the group to counterattacks. This difference is notable because it reveals the potential weaknesses that groups experience as they expand their strategy and shift their tactics and objectives.

---

[44]Jaber (1997).

[45]Wege (1994, p. 157); Nelan (1993, pp. 32–33).

[46]Magnus Ranstorp, "Hezbollah's Future?" *Jane's Intelligence Review*, February 1, 1995.

[47]Wege (1994, p. 157); Nelan (1993, pp. 32–33).

Observations

Like the case study of the Shining Path, this brief assessment of Hizballah's development provides some interesting insights into terrorist groups' potential evolutionary trajectories. Notably, Hizballah did not develop linearly along our capabilities thresholds (discussed in Chapter Two) as the Shining Path did. Instead, the group "skipped" a number of steps, progressing from a collection of unorganized and unsophisticated militias to posing a significant threat in a matter of just two to three years. One of the key factors that enabled this rapid development was the training that Hizballah received from external sources, namely the Iranian Revolutionary Guards. This observation is not particularly new or revolutionary; terrorism experts have long understood the dynamics of state-sponsored terrorism. However, in the context of our capabilities framework, this analysis clarifies the role of external support. The analysis shows that militants can expand and develop sophisticated capabilities on their own but also emphasizes that external support can help them to skip stages and develop more rapidly.

The Hizballah case is also noteworthy in that the group managed to avoid the rapid deterioration experienced by the Shining Path. A significant factor in its success was Hizballah's ability to maintain its support base in southern Lebanon. Even after Israel's withdrawal in 2000, Hizballah continues to play a role in Lebanese politics and has transformed itself into an active political party.[48] In addition to the advantage of training, support from Iran allowed Hizballah to sustain its charitable activities. The Shining Path likewise had access to substantial funds from its participation in the drug trade. The key difference between the two is that Hizballah, wisely, placed a higher priority on maintaining its popular support base than did the Shining Path. Moreover, Hizballah's overall organizational structure allowed for promotion within the group, and thus Hizballah could survive Israel's counterattacks on its leadership when a leader was lost.

Notably, Hizballah did not evidence a substantial shift in its objectives or overall strategy vis-à-vis Israel. Nor did it have to take on the more difficult operational security and command and control

---

[48]Twelve Hizballah members currently participate in the Lebanese parliament.

requirements of an urban insurgency. These factors had less to do with Israeli counterattacks than it did the internal dynamics of the group. Moreover, this case study, as compared with the Shining Path, demonstrates that militant groups are particularly vulnerable to changes in counterterrorism policy as they go through periods of transition.

EGYPTIAN ISLAMIC JIHAD

Egyptian Islamic Jihad began in the late 1970s as a loosely organized group of Muslim Brotherhood supporters and university students opposed to Egypt's secular government.[49] In the early 1980s, the group focused its terrorist acts on government officials, a campaign that began with the 1981 assassination of Egyptian President Anwar Sadat.[50] This incident led to a massive crackdown by Egyptian police and security forces, which imprisoned many members while others fled the country.[51]

A large pool of EIJ members went to Afghanistan following the crackdown, where they received additional training in guerrilla tactics and joined the mujahideen against the Soviet invasion of that country. During this period, in the mid- to late 1980s, the group's campaign against the Egyptian government was at a virtual standstill.[52] Following the end of the Soviet-Afghan war, however, EIJ veterans of the conflict filtered back into Egypt and were able to revitalize their terrorist campaign. The training and experience these cadres had received in guerrilla tactics, operational coordination, and explosive and small arms training while in Afghanistan led the EIJ to renew its strategy of conducting assassinations of government officials and car bombings, several of which succeeded.[53]

---

[49]Sharia law encompasses the rules by which the Muslim world is governed, and the Koran is the principal source of Sharia law.

[50]International Policy Institute for Counter-Terrorism, "Jihad Group," n.d. www.ict. org.il/inter_ter/orgdet.cfm?orgid=18 (accessed September 2003).

[51]International Policy Institute for Counter-Terrorism (n.d.).

[52]Lawrence Wright, "The Man Behind Bin Laden," *The New Yorker*, September 16, 2002, pp. 68–70.

[53]Federation of American Scientists, "Al-Jihad," at www.fas.org/irp/world/para/jihad. htm (accessed August 2003).

Despite initial success, the EIJ's operational expertise was still not substantial enough to pose a serious threat to the stability of the central government in the face of continued Egyptian security crackdowns. Nor was the EIJ able to compete with the larger al-Gama'at al-Islamiyya, or "Islamic Group," for recruits and support within Egypt.[54] The EIJ also lacked a significant base of popular support because it did not make a strong effort to cultivate this support in Cairo, where most of the group's operations occurred. Moreover, the group was viewed by many in the Cairo's mainstream Muslim population as a radical fringe. The EIJ's traditional base of support was in rural Upper Egypt; many in the area lived in extreme poverty and did not have means of supporting the EIJ, nor perhaps did they have an understanding of what the group was trying to accomplish in Cairo. In addition, those who may have wanted to join or provide support to EIJ may have been dissuaded by the heavy-handed tactics used by the government to crack down on the group. As a result of these difficulties, a large group of EIJ members again left Egypt in 1993 with the intent to change their strategy from attacking Egyptian officials inside Egypt to attacking them abroad. The EIJ established cells in Europe and Asia to accomplish this task.[55] This strategy enjoyed some success; in 1995, the EIJ conducted a suicide bombing of the Egyptian embassy in Islamabad, Pakistan, killing 16 and injuring 60.[56] However, the group's leader, Ayman al-Zawahiri, had larger plans for the group.

Al-Zawahiri, who fled Egypt in 1993, met and befriended Osama bin Laden in Sudan.[57] At this time, bin Laden was in the process of establishing al Qaeda to instigate jihad against the United States and Israel. Bin Laden discovered that al-Zawahiri shared his ambitions of waging a worldwide jihad against Israel and the West. This friendship

---

[54]Geneive Abdo, *No God but God: Egypt and the Triumph of Islam*, New York: Oxford University Press, 2000, p. 20. The IG has been responsible for a number of terrorist attacks in Egypt, including the Luxor massacre of 1997.

[55]Wright (2002, p. 78).

[56]The numbers are taken from the International Policy Institute for Counter-Terrorism online database of terrorist attacks. The institute is based in Herzliya, Israel (for more information, see www.ict.org.il).

[57]T. Christian Miller, "The Alleged Brains Behind Bin Laden," *Los Angeles Times*, October 2, 2001.

and the group's eventual incorporation into al Qaeda would become a key transition for the EIJ.

When international sanctions forced bin Laden to abandon Sudan for Afghanistan in 1996, al-Zawahiri went with him to help him run al Qaeda. Two years later, in February 1998, bin Laden released his vision of worldwide jihad against the United States and Israel in the form of a *fatwa*,[58] calling on all Muslims to attack U.S. civilians worldwide. The leaders of four Islamic terrorist groups, including al-Zawahiri, joined in founding the "World Islamic Front for Jihad Against the Jews and Crusaders" by signing this fatwa.

This event redefined the EIJ. Al-Zawahiri's action tied his group to bin Laden's global war against the West, a radical change in orientation for a group whose foremost goal had always been to overthrow the secular Egyptian government. Indeed, al-Zawahiri's decision fomented substantial discord within the EIJ, as many of the group's rank and file preferred to maintain their focus on Egypt.[59] In the end, however, al-Zawahiri prevailed and the EIJ began to reorient itself against Western, particularly U.S., targets.[60]

The EIJ's support for al Qaeda included participating in al Qaeda operations and training new recruits in guerrilla warfare and other terrorist tactics in the group's Afghan camps.[61] In return, bin Laden provided the EIJ with money and other material support, as well as opportunities for more-advanced terrorist training.[62] Indeed, EIJ is believed to have helped plan the 1998 double suicide car bombing of U.S. embassies in Kenya and Tanzania, which killed 258 and injured thousands, and the group attempted an attack on the U.S. embassy in Albania later the same year.[63] Al-Zawahiri also has played a key role in planning subsequent al Qaeda attacks, including those on

---

[58]Islamic religious ruling, or decision.

[59]Anonymous (2002, p. 172).

[60]Wright (2002, p. 83).

[61]Judy Aita, "Ali Mohamed: The Defendant Who Did Not Go to Trial," *International Information Programs* [U.S. Department of State], May 15, 2001.

[62]Aita (2001).

[63]These numbers are from U.S. Information Agency, "U.S. Court Document Links Bombing Suspect to Bin Ladin Organization," press release, August 28, 1998. The Albania operation was thwarted.

September 11, 2001. In the wake of the 1998 attacks, U.S. and other security services arrested a number of senior EIJ members involved in these plots.[64] Moreover, security services around the globe dismantled entire EIJ cells.[65]

In response to this pressure, the EIJ stepped up recruiting efforts and dispersed to safer areas, such as Iran and Lebanon.[66] Moreover, internal tensions within the group increased as well, as those who had opposed the shift away from the EIJ's original goals rebelled. In 1999, the rank-and-file members opposed to al-Zawahiri's relationship with bin Laden won a 1999 vote to oust al-Zawahiri as EIJ leader.[67] However, throughout 1999, the group continued to experience difficulties conducting operations against Egyptian targets abroad and as a result asked al-Zawahiri to return as leader in 2000.[68] As a final act of solidarity with bin Laden, al-Zawahiri formalized the EIJ's relationship with al Qaeda by agreeing to officially merge the two groups in June 2001.[69] At this writing, al-Zawahiri, who is widely considered to be bin Laden's top lieutenant and a key strategist behind al Qaeda operations, is still at large, while EIJ has largely been subsumed within the al Qaeda network.[70]

Observations

The EIJ's evolutionary trajectory, while distinct from Hizballah and Shining Path, demonstrates some important commonalities with these groups. With regard to the capability thresholds, much like Hizballah, the EIJ "skipped" several steps. It went from an unorganized group of university students with radical ideas to striking a

---

[64]Jailan Halawi, "Militants Handed Over," *Al-Ahram Weekly*, No. 427, April 29–May 5, 1999.

[65]U.S. Department of State, *Patterns of Global Terrorism*, 1999, Appendix B, www.state.gov/www/global/terrorism/1999report/appb.html.

[66]Federation of American Scientists, "Al-Jihad."

[67]Abduh Zaynah, "Report on Ayman Al-Zawahiri's Life, Connection with Bin Laden," *Al-Sharq al-Awsat*, September 22, 2001.

[68]Wright (2002, p. 83).

[69]U.S. Department of State (1999, p. 105).

[70]See Ed Blanche, "Ayman Al-Zawahiri: Attention Turns to the Other Prime Suspect," *Jane's Intelligence Review*, October 3, 2001.

guarded target, the prime minister, as its first act of terror. Because this strategy worked so well for the EIJ the first time, the group focused on attacking guarded targets almost exclusively during its active phase in Egypt and prior to its merger with al Qaeda. It is likely that the EIJ chose this strategy partly by design and partly because of an inability to improve its capabilities on its own. Surprisingly, the EIJ's experience in Afghanistan of fighting a guerrilla war against the Soviets gave the group additional skills, but it did not appear to translate into an increased capability to conduct terrorist attacks in Egypt. The EIJ demonstrated its ability to intentionally strike at unguarded foreign nationals, kill or injure more than 150 in a single attack, and conduct multiple attacks once it joined forces with al Qaeda and acquired additional training and resources, all of which occurred outside Egypt. Much like Hizballah and the Abu Sayyaf Group (discussed in the next section), the EIJ's relationship with al Qaeda served as a force multiplier for the group and also enabled it to operate at higher thresholds of capability than when the group was on its own.

In terms of anti-U.S. sentiment, the EIJ went from displaying no real anti-U.S. sentiment as part of its rhetoric to absorbing all three thresholds almost immediately upon joining forces with al Qaeda. Although internal dissent within the group over al-Zawahiri's decision to take on the United States as a target initially divided the EIJ, the group's inability to attack Egyptian targets on its own after removing al-Zawahiri as leader resulted in the eventual decision a year later to join al Qaeda and attack U.S. targets.

Perhaps most importantly, the lack of popular support for its campaign led to the EIJ's demise in Egypt. Although while in Egypt the group displayed a high threshold of capability and executed some successful attacks, the EIJ was never able to gain momentum there due in large part to the lack of popular support. The group remained unable to recruit new members, and its small size made government crackdowns devastating with no ready replacements available to fill in leadership positions following widespread arrests. The EIJ also was unable to improve its capabilities because it lacked a pool of supporters to provide arms, financial support, or an operational space to train.

The EIJ case study shows that this small but capable terrorist group was only able to survive imminent demise by leaving its immediate area of operation, establishing a widespread international network, and merging with a stronger, more robust terrorist organization. Conversely, the ASG, as we will discuss in the next section, still faces imminent demise even after it forged a relationship with al Qaeda because much like the EIJ it is small and capable. But unlike the EIJ, the ASG remains primarily in its immediate geographic area of operation.

ABU SAYYAF GROUP

The Abu Sayyaf Group is an Islamic terrorist group operating in Mindanao, a province in the southern Philippines. Abdurajak Janjalani established the ASG in 1991 as a breakaway faction of the Moro National Liberation Front, which was a nationalist insurgent group that had been engaged in guerrilla warfare against the Philippine government since the 1960s.[71] The MNLF negotiated a peace settlement with the Philippine government in 1996, eventually establishing the Autonomous Region of Muslim Mindanao.[72] But the ASG rejects this resolution. Its stated purpose is to overthrow the secular, Christian-dominated government and replace it with an Islamic state in Mindanao and the Sulu Archipelago.[73]

In comparison to the SL or Hizballah, the ASG has maintained a smaller membership, approximately 500 members at the height of its strength in the late 1990s.[74] Between 1991 and 1998 the militant

---

[71]Kim Cragin and Peter Chalk, *Terrorism & Development: Using Social and Economic Development to Inhibit a Resurgence of Terrorism*, Santa Monica, Calif.: RAND Corporation, MR-1630-RC, 2003, pp. 15–22. See also "Abu Sayyaf," *Jane's Terrorism Intelligence*, March 4, 2003, and Robert Reid, "The Philippines' Abu Sayyaf: Bandits or International Terrorists?" Associated Press, April 6, 1995.

[72]Cragin and Chalk (2003); "Abu Sayyaf" (2003); Reid (1995).

[73]Cragin and Chalk (2003); "Abu Sayyaf" (2003); Reid (1995).

[74]In comparison, the MILF maintains approximately 35,000 members. See Andrew Tan, "Armed Muslim Separatist Rebellion in Southeast Asia: Persistence, Prospects, and Implications," *Studies in Conflict and Terrorism*, Vol. 23, 2000, pp. 267–288; "Soldiers Capture Main Camp of Rebel Abu Sayyaf Group," *BBC News* [online], July 19, 1997; "Abu Sayyaf Will Take Over a Year to Regroup," *BusinessWorld*, December 23, 1998; and author interview, Philippine security officials, Manila, 2002.

group began to expand and develop its capabilities, moving from a group able to conduct a small attack to successfully targeting foreign nationals. For example, in the first years of the ASG's campaign, the group mostly kidnapped local residents, bombed churches in the area, or killed local Christian residents.[75] The ASG could sustain this level of capability because many of its members were drawn from the pools of disgruntled former-MNLF or Islamic insurgent Moro Islamic Liberation Front fighters.[76] Moreover, many MILF and ASG cadre fought in Afghanistan against the Soviets during the 1980s, learning guerrilla tactics they could use to fight Islamic insurgencies at home.[77]

The ASG increased its capabilities in the mid-1990s, using external support from Osama bin Laden and his jihad network. For example, in the early 1990s, bin Laden sent foreign mujahideen to the Philippines to train select ASG members.[78] In addition to this training, bin Laden also directed his brother-in-law, Mohammad Jamal Khalifa, to set up training networks in the southern Philippines through Islamic charities.[79] Pakistani terrorist Ramzi Yousef, responsible for the World Trade Center bombing in 1993, also reportedly trained ASG rebels in the early 1990s on the use of sophisticated high explosives.[80] Finally, the ASG was able to access money and weapons from external sources, including bin Laden, as well as from underground networks in Pakistan, Malaysia, and Vietnam.[81]

The interaction that the ASG had with bin Laden's network influenced both its capabilities and intentions. The ASG shifted its target selection at that time and began to focus its attacks on U.S. and Saudi

---

[75]"Abu Sayyaf" (2003).

[76]Reid (1995); Tan (2000, pp. 267–288).

[77]For more information on the presence of Southeast Asian Muslim fighters in Afghanistan, see John McBeth, "The Danger Within," *Far Eastern Economic Review,* September 27, 2001, and Lira Dalangin, "Bin Laden Kin Denies Hand in RP Terror Cells," *INQ7.net,* May 15, 2002.

[78]Rigoberto Tiglao, "To Fight or Not to Fight," *Far Eastern Economic Review,* March 9, 1999; Tan (2000, pp. 267–288).

[79]Rigoberto Tiglao, "Terror International: Manila Claims Foreign Groups Support Extremists," *Far Eastern Economic Review,* May 4, 1995.

[80]Tan (2000, p. 275).

[81]Tan (2000).

targets. For example, in 1993, the ASG kidnapped an American from his home in the Philippines and held him for three weeks.[82] At the same time, the ASG also demonstrated an increase in its capabilities. The group conducted an attack on a Philippine airliner and bombed a church in December 1994, killing six and injuring 130.[83]

The ASG experienced a significant setback in December 1998, however, when its founder and leader Janjalani was killed in a shoot-out with Philippine forces.[84] Janjalani's death devastated the group, as he had played a key role in maintaining the ASG's cohesion, strategy, and tactics. Following this leadership change, the group split into several factions, each with a separate leadership and agenda.[85] In addition to changes within the group's internal structure, external support to the ASG declined temporarily after Janjalani's death.[86] This decline stemmed from the group's uncertain future and its increased focus on conducting largely criminal acts, such as taking hostages for ransom, which had little to do with the broader ideological aims of ASG's supporters.[87] In an attempt to recover its losses following Janjalani's death, the ASG decided to grab world attention by focusing more on hostage taking of U.S. and Western civilians.[88] It appears that the ASG hoped to gain funding through the payment of ransom, in addition to regalvanizing support from Islamic terrorist financiers, including bin Laden.[89]

Currently, the ASG faces an intensified counterterrorism campaign by the Philippine government. This campaign has accelerated with U.S. military training and support. As a result, the ASG has suffered at

---

[82]For more information, see the RAND Terrorism Chronology (http://db.mipt.org).

[83]RAND Terrorism Chronology (http://db.mipt.org).

[84]"Abu Sayyaf Will Take over a Year to Regroup" (1998); "Who Are the Abu Sayyaf?" *BBC News* [online], June 1, 2001.

[85]"Who Are the Abu Sayyaf?" (2001).

[86]"Profile: Abu Sayyaf," *Online NewsHour*, January 2002.

[87]Center for Defense Information, "In the Spotlight: Abu Sayyaf," CDI Terrorism Project, March 5, 2002a.

[88]Center for Defense Information (2002a).

[89]For more information, see U.S. Department of Justice, "Six Additional Members of the Abu Sayyaf Group Indicted in Connection with Hostage-Taking and Murder of Americans and Others in the Philippines," press release, December 10, 2002.

least a short-term decrease in effectiveness since this campaign began, and prospects for the group's long-term success are in question.[90]

Observations

The Abu Sayyaf Group adds an additional dimension to our analysis because its evolutionary trajectory is both shorter (time frame) and smaller (with regard to capabilities) than the other groups studied. Over a period of approximately five years, the ASG moved from having the ability to conduct any attack to having the capacity to target foreign nationals. The primary factor that contributed to this increase was the ASG's interaction with the MILF and with al Qaeda. Both of these Islamic organizations provided the ASG with training, similar to how the Iranian Revolutionary Guards provided training to Hizballah.

The ASG, however, never reached the level of capability of Hizballah. A number of factors account for this difference. For example, Hizballah did not need to compete with another, larger insurgency for recruitment pools, weapons, money, or control over territory. In contrast, the ASG operated in the shadow of the larger MILF, another Islamic insurgency that gained substantial credibility with Mindanao Muslims. The same could be said for the EIJ and its relationship with al-Gamat, which explained, in part, why the EIJ began to operate outside Egypt. Thus, the ASG's relationship with other militant groups, such as al Qaeda and the Indonesian Islamic extremist group Jemaah Islamiya, may be driven by a need to compete with the MILF for credibility and strength in Mindanao. In addition, the death of Janjalani clearly had a negative impact on the ASG. Not only did the group lose its ideologue, but Janjalani's loss also resulted in the group fracturing. Each of these factors is likely to have limited the expansion and development of the ASG.

---

[90]"Airport Bomb: Islamic Group Blamed," *CNN.com*, March 6, 2003. However, at the time of this writing, although the ASG is still active, the MILF has also begun conducting operations in the Philippines even though it had been observing a cease-fire since 2001.

More importantly, the ASG's relationship with al Qaeda apparently influenced a shift in its objectives, as the ASG began to attack U.S. and other Western targets. This shift demonstrates the impact that other like-minded organizations can have on insurgent groups, especially if these external organizations provide funding. As with the EIJ, Osama bin Laden provided aid to the ASG, and this aid also shifted the group's evolutionary trajectory.

RISING UP AND FALLING DOWN: TERRORIST GROUPS IN TRANSITION

This chapter provides some insight into how militant organizations respond to changes in their internal and external environments. The result is four different narratives that outline the evolutionary trajectories of these groups and, more importantly, demonstrate how terrorist groups adapt and change. Moreover, they refine our threat framework. Figure 2.3 in Chapter Two identified a hypothetical mapping of changes as al Qaeda cadres migrate; however, the analysis included in this chapter allows us to deepen our understanding of these potential shifts. To illustrate how this discussion fits into the context of our framework, the following figures (4.1–4.3) chart the evolutionary trajectories over time of the four groups analyzed in this chapter.

Interestingly, although the groups developed in different environments, faced different counterattacks by state authorities, and articulated different objectives, our analysis discovered some similarities in their trajectories. We, therefore, argue that understanding these similarities is an important component of designing effective counterterrorism policies. For example, all four groups responded and adjusted to counterattacks by state authorities, although some more successfully than others. Similarly, the case studies illustrate that

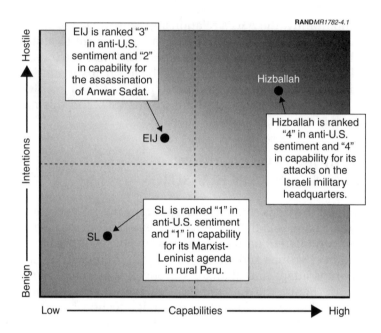

Figure 4.1—Mapping the Threats Posed by Four Terrorist
Groups in 1982

external support (from states or other militant organizations) can
affect groups' capabilities and intentions. Finally, all four cases highlight how militant groups are vulnerable to the loss of popular support. While none of these points is revolutionary on its own, together
they lead us to the following conclusion: Terrorist groups in transition are particularly vulnerable, especially if actions taken against
them magnify the pressures forcing the evolution.

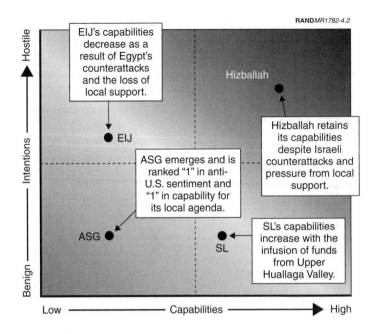

Figure 4.2—Mapping the Threats Posed by Four Terrorist Groups in 1992

In part, one would expect this to be true simply because *change implies uncertainty*. When groups are in transition, they face choices—choices about their own organizational structures, about strategy, and about tactics. If they choose poorly, the results can be devastating. Appreciating the pressures for change that may be at work on a group may help authorities apply complementary measures that, as a result, increase the chances of the terrorists making bad decisions.

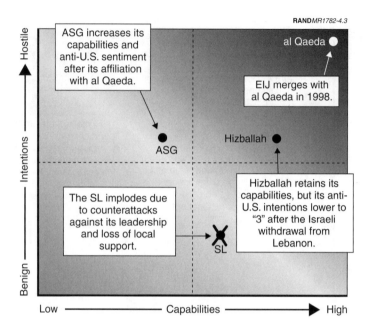

Figure 4.3—Mapping the Threats Posed by Four Terrorist Groups in 2002

Chapter Five

CONCLUSION

The September 11, 2001, attacks on the World Trade Center and the Pentagon illustrate the difficulty in forecasting new and emerging trends in terrorism. The intelligence and security communities clearly were tracking the activities of Osama bin Laden and his "World Islamic Front for Jihad Against the Jews and Crusaders" long before September 11. This was shown, for example, when the U.S. government conducted retaliatory missile strikes against bin Laden's group in Afghanistan and Sudan in 1998. Yet many members of the counterterrorism community appear to have underestimated either the network's degree of hostility toward the United States or its capabilities; more importantly, the lethal combination of the two also appears to have been underestimated.

In making this observation, we are not attempting to critique the U.S. security community or terrorism analysis in general. Rather, it is our belief that the very nature of terrorism poses a significant part of the problem. As Bruce Hoffman stated in his book, *Inside Terrorism*, "The terrorist campaign is like a shark in the water: it must keep moving forward—no matter how slowly or incrementally—or die."[1] Conceptually, the United States faces a terrorist threat that is beyond al Qaeda or any other single group in existence today. It confronts the U.S. government with the need to protect its citizens from a collection of different militant organizations that evidence varying degrees of hostility toward the United States and an ability to attack U.S. interests. More importantly, the composition of this threat could

---

[1]Hoffman (1998, p. 162).

change tomorrow. As a result of this fluidity, we have attempted, in this report, to generate a framework that allows policymakers and terrorism analysts to place parameters around the threat, without compromising its dynamic nature.

The tension between bounding the threat for policymakers and not losing too much of the flexibility that terrorism analysis requires exists throughout this entire report. Moreover, we argue that it is this tension that contributes the most to the existing terrorism literature today, which deals with the unstated issue by either focusing on one particular terrorist group (and, hence, any policy recommendations apply only to that group at that particular time) or generalizing terrorism trends to such a degree that little useful policy prescription can be taken from the analysis. RAND terrorism analysts have attempted to bridge this gap for the past 30 years—a clear example being Ian Lesser et al.'s *Countering the New Terrorism*, published in 1999. Similarly, a report by Bonnie Cordes et al., *A Conceptual Framework for Analyzing Terrorist Groups*, published in 1985, also attempted to bring academic terrorism analysis together with policy requirements to aid U.S. decisionmakers.[2] In this context, we view this report as one step further in providing policymakers with a useful tool for identifying and understanding new and emerging threats in terrorism.

Clearly, much more needs to be done. In this report, we provide only an initial assessment of what factors—internal and external—cause militant organizations to adjust over time. These shifts are key for counterterrorism policy because they highlight decisionmaking within terrorist groups and reveal potential vulnerabilities that can be exploited. Our preliminary findings need to be explored more thoroughly, however, with additional empirical research. Similarly, it might be interesting to look at ongoing shifts in the context of the war on terrorism, examining how terrorist groups have reacted to an intense global campaign led by the U.S. government and its allies. In addition, this report examines the threats posed to U.S. interests worldwide, but it would also be useful to adjust the framework to

---

[2]Cordes, Bonnie, Brian Michael Jenkins, Konrad Kellen, Gail V. Bass-Golod, Daniel A. Relles, William F. Sater, Mario L. Juncosa, William Fowler, and Geraldine Petty, *A Conceptual Framework for Analyzing Terrorist Groups*, Santa Monica, Calif.: RAND Corporation, R-3151, 1985.

focus on threats to the U.S. homeland specifically. Finally, it should be noted that we focus intentionally on the organizational and operational requirements that affect militant organizations' *capabilities*. For the purposes of this analysis, we have set aside a more thorough assessment of intentions and motivations. Yet such an assessment clearly affects any "hearts and minds" campaign the U.S. government might undertake to reduce recruitment or lessen general popular support for terrorists' goals. These issues are just a few of the many challenges faced by policymakers as they attempt to design counterterrorism policy. As such, this particular report should be interpreted in this wider context, as one of many steps toward developing and sustaining an effective counterterrorism strategy.

TRENDS IN TERRORIST ATTACKS

Chapter Two outlined our threat framework in the context of anti-U.S. sentiment and attack capabilities. This appendix provides more information on the historical trends in terrorist attacks in order to set the context for our attack capability thresholds. These thresholds are as follows:

1. the demonstrated ability to kill or injure more than 50 people in a single attack over the past five years (or since 1998)

2. the demonstrated ability to target foreign nationals over the past five years (or since 1998)

3. the demonstrated or perceived ability to kill or injure more than 150 people in a single attack over the past five years

4. the demonstrated or perceived ability to attack well-guarded targets successfully over the past five years

5. the demonstrated or perceived ability to conduct multiple, co-ordinated attacks across time and space successfully over the past five years.

From 1998 through 2002, RAND's database recorded 1,028 international terrorist attacks, yet only 60 of those meet the thresholds listed above. In this period, terrorists averaged approximately one death and three injuries per attack; this average *includes* the September 11, 2001, attacks. Yet we determined, for this framework, that we wanted to be able to isolate the groups that pose the most significant threat to the United States. We therefore chose "cause 50 casualties" as a purposefully high threshold. Moreover, just because a group demonstrates its ability to cross a threshold does not mean than *every single attack* likewise crosses the same threshold. For example, Hizballah has demonstrated its ability to attack guarded targets successfully. But this does not mean that every attack by Hizballah on guarded targets is successful or that every attack reaches this threshold. Hizballah conducts numerous attacks that do not reach even the first "kill or injure 50 people" threshold. Figure A.1 illustrates these 60 attacks, which are divided according to our capability indicators.

It is clear from this figure that our capability indicators do illustrate a progression of capabilities. However, we note in the report that it is difficult to separate out a particular terrorist group's intentions to *target*, for example, foreign nationals from an inadvertent foreign casualty in a local terrorist attack. In Figure A.2, we demonstrate this difference by comparing patterns of attacks in which U.S. citizens or businesses were the secondary targets with those when U.S. citizens or foreign nationals were specifically surveyed or "cased" and attacked.

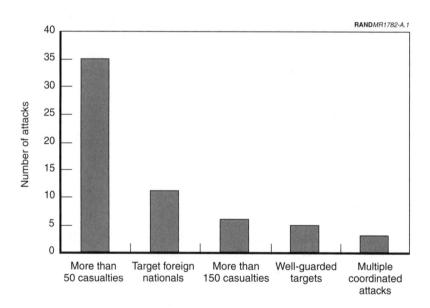

Figure A.1—Terrorist Attacks According to Five Capability Thresholds, 1998–2000

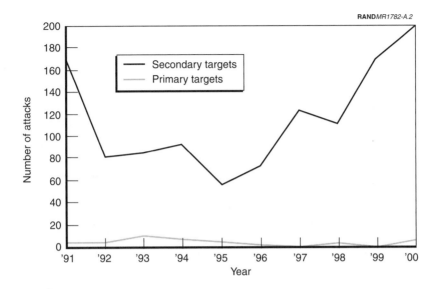

RAND*MR1782-A.2*

Figure A.2—Intentional vs. Inadvertent Attacks on Foreign Nationals

Finally, it is interesting to compare our two casualty "capability indicators" over time. Figure A.3 shows a clear distinction between attacks that cause more than 50 casualties and attacks that kill or injure more than 150 people. Some experts have argued that terrorists want a lot of people watching and listening, but not a lot of deaths—hence, the common perception, mentioned in Chapter One, of "terrorism as theater." Figure A.3 demonstrates how the lethality of terrorist attacks also has fluctuated over the past decade.

We emphasize that the historical data above are by no means intended to be used as an indicator of future terrorist attacks. But rather, we included these data to provide context to the thresholds that we picked for the analytical framework presented in Chapter Two. Clearly, other thresholds could equally serve as indicators of terrorist group capabilities—with lower thresholds to provide an overall measure of terrorists' abilities or higher thresholds to provide indicators of groups' abilities to attack the U.S. homeland. Yet we believe that these thresholds are useful metrics for assessing terrorist capabilities against each other—even in a highly dynamic and changing world.

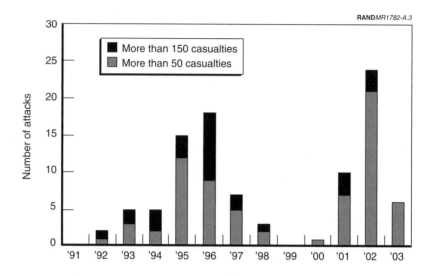

Figure A.3—Patterns in Lethality of Terrorist Attacks

BIBLIOGRAPHY

Abdo, Geneive, *No God but God: Egypt and the Triumph of Islam*, New York: Oxford University Press, 2000.

Abu-Amr, Ziad, *Islamic Fundamentalism in the West Bank and Gaza*, Bloomington, Ind.: Indiana University Press, 1994.

"Abu Sayyaf," *Jane's Terrorism Intelligence*, March 4, 2003.

"Abu Sayyaf Will Take Over a Year to Regroup," *BusinessWorld*, December 23, 1998.

Ahmad, Munir, "Christian Leaders Refuse to Bow to Terror," *Washington Times*, August 11, 2002.

"Airport Bomb: Islamic Group Blamed," *CNN.com*, March 6, 2003, http://edition.cnn.com/2003/WORLD/asiapcf/southeast/03/06/p hilippines.bomb/index.html (accessed August 2003).

Aita, Judy, "Ali Mohamed: The Defendant Who Did Not Go to Trial," *International Information Programs* [U.S. Department of State], May 15, 2001, http://usinfo.state.gov/topical/pol/terror/010515 02.htm.

_____, "U.S. Completes Presentation of Evidence in Embassy Bombing Trial," U.S. Department of State, Office of International Information Programs, http://usinfo.state.gov/regional/af/securi ty/a1040558.htm, n.d. (accessed September 2003).

"Al-Jihad," http://library.nps.navy.mil/home/tgp/jihad.htm, (accessed September 2003) (profile from U.S. Department of State, *Patterns of Global Terrorism*, 2002).

"Al-Qaeda May Use Internet to Regroup," *BBC News*, March 6, 2002.

"Al-Qaeda Suspect Filmed WTC," *CNN.com*, July 16, 2002.

Alterman, Jon B., "The Luxor Shootout and Egypt's Armed Islamist Opposition," *Policywatch*, No. 279, November 17, 1997.

Anonymous, *Through Our Enemies Eyes*, Washington, D.C: Brassey's, 2002.

Aponte, Eliana, "Car Bomb in Bogota Kills 32," *USA Today*, February 8, 2003, www.usatoday.com/news/world/2003-02-07-colombia-explosion_x.htm (accessed August 2003).

"Armas por Coca," *Cambio*, July 12, 1999.

"Army Reports Heavy Child Involvement in Guerrilla War," *El País*, December 27, 2000.

Arnson, Cynthia, ed., *Comparative Peace Processes in Latin America*, Washington, D.C.: Woodrow Wilson Center Press, 1999.

"Baalbek Seen as Staging Area for Terrorism," *Washington Post*, January 9, 1984.

Bandura, Albert, "Mechanisms of Moral Disengagement," in Reich (1998).

Basombrío, Carlos, "Peace in Peru: An Unfinished Task," in Arnson (1999).

"La Batalla de Córdoba," *Cambio*, May 24, 1999.

Bedi, R., "'Red Terror' Gaining Ground in Nepal," *Jane's Terrorism and Security Monitor*, July 2, 2002.

Belfast Agreement, accessible online at www.ofmdfmni.gov.uk/publications/ba.htm (accessed September 2003)

Bell, J. Bowyer, "Revolutionary Dynamics: The Inherent Inefficiency of the Underground," *Terrorism and Political Violence*, Vol. 2, No. 4, 1990.

_____, *IRA Tactics and Targets: An Analysis of Tactical Aspects of the Armed Struggle 1969–1989*, New Brunswick, N.J.: Transaction Publishers, 1991.

_____, *The IRA 1968–2000: An Analysis of a Secret Army*, London: Frank Cass, 2000.

Bergen, Peter, *Holy War, Inc.: Inside the Secret World of Osama Bin Laden*, New York: The Free Press, 2001.

Black, Ian, and Benny Morris, *Israel's Secret Wars: A History of Israel's Intelligence Services*, New York: Grove Weidenfeld, 1991.

Blanche, Ed, "Ayman Al-Zawahiri: Attention Turns to the Other Prime Suspect," *Jane's Intelligence Review*, October 3, 2001.

Bonner, Raymond, and Jane Perlez, "Find Cleric Linked to Al-Qaeda, U.S. Urges," *New York Times*, February 19, 2002.

Bowen, Sally, "Peru Rebel Chief 'Seeks Peace Deal,'" *Financial Times*, October 2, 1993.

Boyne, Sean, "The Real IRA: After Omagh, What Now?" *Jane's Intelligence Review*, August 24, 1998.

"Britain and Ireland Issue a Plan for Full Talks on Ulster," *New York Times*, February 23, 1995.

Brodzinsky, Sibylla, "U.S. Crosses a Line in Colombia," *MSNBC*, February 14, 2003, at www.msnbc.com/news/705583.asp (accessed August 2003).

Brooke, James, "Snaring the Top Guerrilla: 'Bingo! We Got Him,'" *New York Times*, September 15, 1992.

Buchanan, Michael, "Europe's Hunt for Al-Qaeda," *BBC News* [online], September 6, 2002, http://news.bbc.co.uk/1/low/world/europe/2240867.stm (accessed August 2003).

Bush, George W., Remarks by the President on Financial Aspects of Terrorism, December 20, 2001, at http://www.whitehouse.gov/news/releases/2001/12/20011220-11.html (accessed August 2003).

Center for Defense Information, "In the Spotlight: Abu Sayyaf," CDI Terrorism Project, March 5, 2002a, www.cdi.org/terrorism/sayyaf.cfm (accessed September 2003).

_____, "In the Spotlight: Laskar Jihad," CDI Terrorism Project, March 8, 2002b, www.cdi.org/terrorism/laskar-pr.cfm (accessed September 2003).

"Cheap and Trusted," *The Economist*, November 22, 2001.

Chernick, Marc, "Negotiating Peace Amid Multiple Forms of Violence," in Arnson (1999).

Chew, Amy, "Indonesia Pressures Islamic Militias," *CNN.com*, October 31, 2002, at http://www.cnn.com/2002/WORLD/asiapcf/southeast/10/31/indonesia.crackdown/ (accessed August 2003).

"Clerics May Have Stoked Radicals' Fire: Qaeda Said to Use Some Radical Clerics to Help Its Cause," *Boston Globe*, August 4, 2002.

"Colombia Blasts Kill 13 as Uribe Takes Office," *CNN.com*, August 8, 2002.

Coogan, Tim Pat, *The IRA: A History*, Niwot, Colorado: Rinehart Publishers, 1993.

_____, *The Troubles: Ireland's Ordeal, 1965–1995, and the Search for Peace*, London: Hutchinson, 1995.

Cordes, Bonnie, Brian Michael Jenkins, Konrad Kellen, Gail V. Bass-Golod, Daniel A. Relles, William F. Sater, Mario L. Juncosa, William Fowler, and Geraldine Petty, *A Conceptual Framework for Analyzing Terrorist Groups*, Santa Monica, Calif.: RAND Corporation, R-3151, 1985.

"Corkman in Charge as Real IRA Threat Remains," *Irish Times*, May 24, 2001.

"Los Costos del Cese al Fuego," *El País*, July 6, 2000.

Cowan, Rosie, "Real IRA 'Ready to Attack,'" *Guardian Unlimited*, October 21, 2002.

CPRS Public Opinion Poll No. 22, accessed at http://www.pcpsr.org/survey/cprspolls/96/poll22c.html#armpeace (accessed August 2003).

Cragin, Kim, and Peter Chalk, *Terrorism & Development: Using Social and Economic Development to Inhibit a Resurgence of Terrorism*, Santa Monica, Calif.: RAND Corporation, MR-1630-RC, 2003.

Crenshaw, Martha, ed., *Terrorism in Context*, State College, Pa.: Pennsylvania State University Press, 1995.

_____, "The Logic of Terrorism: Terrorist Behavior as a Product of Strategic Choice," in Reich (1998).

Dalangin, Lira, "Bin Laden Kin Denies Hand in RP Terror Cells," *INQ7.net*, May 15, 2002.

Daly, John, "Will Sri Lanka's Peace Accord with the Tamil Tigers Hold?" *Jane's Terrorism and Security Monitor*, April 1, 2002.

Dawoud, Khaled, "Egypt Terror Leaders Renounce Violence," *The Guardian*, August 2, 2002, www.guardian.co.uk/international/story/0,3604,767732,00.html (accessed September 2003).

della Porta, Donatella, "Left-Wing Terrorism in Italy," in Crenshaw (1995).

Dingley, James, "The Bombing on Omagh, 15 August 1998: The Bombers, Their Tactics, Strategy and Purpose Behind the Incident," *Studies in Conflict and Terrorism*, No. 24, 2001.

Eedle, Paul, "Al-Qaeda Takes Fight for 'Hearts and Minds' to the Web," *Jane's Intelligence Review*, August 1, 2002.

Eickelman, Dale F., and Jon W. Anderson, eds., *New Media in the Muslim World*, Bloomington, Ind.: Indiana University Press, 1999.

el-Nawawy, Mohammed, and Adel Iskandar, *Al-Jazeera: How the Free Arab News Network Scooped the World and Changed the Middle East*, Cambridge, Mass.: Westview Press, 2002.

Emerson, Steven, "Meltdown," *The New Republic*, November 23, 1992.

_____, *American Jihad: The Terrorists Living Among Us*, New York: The Free Press, 2002.

Falkenrath, Richard, et al., *America's Achilles' Heel: Nuclear, Biological, and Chemical Terrorism and Covert Attack*, Cambridge, Mass.: MIT Press, 1998.

"Farc se Movilizan al Sur de Bolívar," *El Tiempo*, July 16, 2000.

Farrell, Nick, "US Fears Nuclear Cyber Terror Attacks," *vnunet.com*, June 27, 2002, www.vnunet.com/News/1133033 (accessed September 2003).

Federation of American Scientists, "Al-Jihad," at www.fas.org/irp/world/para/jihad.htm (accessed August 2003).

"Five Hamas Members Nabbed for Hebrew University Bombing," Associated Press, August 22, 2002.

Ganguly, Meenakshi, "A Banking System Built for Terrorism," *Time*, October 5, 2001.

"General Tapias on Puerto Lleras Attack," *Semana*, July 11, 1999.

"German at Center of Sept. 11 Inquiry: Suspect Recruited Hijackers in Hamburg," *Washington Post*, June 12, 2002.

"Glimmering Path," *The Economist*, July 29, 1995.

Gordon, Michael R., "U.S. Is Given Papers That Israelis Assert Tie Arafat to Terror," *New York Times*, April 11, 2002, p. A1.

Gorriti, Gustavo, *The Shining Path: A History of the Millenarian War in Peru*, Robin Kirk (trans.), Chapel Hill, N.C.: University of North Carolina Press, 1999.

Gunaratna, Rohan, *Inside Al Qaeda: Global Network of Terror*, New York: Columbia University Press, 2002.

Halawi, Jailan, "Militants Handed Over," *Al-Ahram Weekly*, No. 427, April 29–May 5, 1999, http://weekly.ahram.org.eg/1999/427/eg7.htm (accessed September 2003).

Harel, Amos, Daniel Sobelman, and Jonathan Lis, "Israeli Officials: Progress in Hezbollah Prisoner Exchange Talks," *Ha'aretz*, July 12, 2002.

Harisumarto, Sukino, "Analysis: Politics of Terrorist Socials," United Press International, June 1, 2002.

Hoffman, Bruce, *Inside Terrorism*, New York: Columbia University Press, 1998.

_____, "The Debate Over Future Terrorist Use of Chemical, Biological, Radiological, and Nuclear Weapons," in Roberts (2000, pp. 215–218).

Hopkins, Nick, and Tania Branigan, "Poison Find Sparks Terror Alert," *Guardian Unlimited*, January 8, 2003.

Hroub, Khaled, *Hamas: Political Thought and Practice*, Washington, D.C.: Institute for Palestine Studies, 2000.

Human Rights Watch, "Suicide Bombing Attacks on Civilians," Chapter 3 of *Erased in a Moment: Suicide Bombing Attacks Against Israeli Civilians*, New York, 2002, www.hrw.org/reports/2002/isrl-pa/ISRAELPA1002-03.htm (accessed September 2003).

International Crisis Group, "Yemen: Coping with Terrorism and Violence in a Fragile State," January 8, 2003.

International Policy Institute for Counter-Terrorism, "Jihad Group," n.d., www.ict.org.il/inter_ter/orgdet.cfm?orgid=18 (accessed September 2003).

Jaber, Hala, *Hezbollah: Born with a Vengeance*, New York: Columbia University Press, 1997.

Jenkins, Brian Michael, "Colombia: Crossing a Dangerous Threshold," *The National Interest*, Winter 2000.

"Jerusalem Blasts Kills 7; 4 Americans Among Dead," *CNN.com*, August 1, 2002.

Johnson, Kevin, and Toni Locy, "Men on Tapes Seem Ready to Die for Al-Qaeda," *USA Today*, January 18, 2002, www.usatoday.com/

news/attack/2002/01/18/usat-suspects.htm#more (accessed September 2003).

Kelley, Jack, "Militants Wire Web with Links to Jihad Islamic Groups," *Newsfactor.com*, July 10, 2002.

Khan, Kamram, and John Lancaster, "Pakistan Holds 3 in U.S. Consulate Bombing," *Washington Post Foreign Service*, July 9, 2002.

Khan, Zarar, "Suicide Bomb Plot Against Americans Foiled," *Washington Times*, December 16, 2002.

Koonings, Kees, and Dirk Kruijt, eds., *Societies of Fear: The Legacy of Civil War, Violence and Terror in Latin America*, London: Zed Books, 1999.

Kotler, Jared, "Guerrillas to Study Curbing the Use of Homemade Missiles," Associated Press, February 13, 2001.

Lesser, Ian O., Bruce Hoffman, John Arquilla, David F. Ronfeldt, and Michele Zanini, *Countering the New Terrorism*, Santa Monica, Calif.: RAND Corporation, MR-989-AF, 1999.

Levitt, Matthew, "Testimony on Behalf of the Washington Institute for Near East Studies," hearing before the House Committee on International Relations regarding the Syrian Accountability Act of 2002, September 18, 2002, http://freelebanon.org/testimonies/t65.htm (accessed September 2003).

MacVicar, Shelia, and Henry Schuster, "European Terror Suspects Got Al Qaeda Training, Sources Say," *CNN.com*, February 6, 2003, www.cnn.com/2003/US/02/06/sprj.irq.alqaeda.links/ (accessed September 2003).

"Man Alleged to Aid 9/11 Cell Arrested in German Inquiry: Moroccan Man Assisted Hamburg Group, Officials Say," *Washington Post*, October 11, 2002.

McBeth, John, "The Danger Within," *Far Eastern Economic Review*, September 27, 2001.

McClintock, Cynthia, *Revolutionary Movements in Latin America: El Salvador's FMLN and Peru's Shining Path*, Washington, D.C.: U.S. Institute of Peace Press, 1998.

_____, "The Decimation of Peru's Sendero Luminoso," in Arnson (1999).

McCormick, Gordon H., *The Shining Path and the Future of Peru*, Santa Monica, Calif.: RAND Corporation, R-3781-DOS/OSD, 1990.

_____, *From the Sierra to the Cities: The Urban Campaign of the Shining Path*, Santa Monica, Calif.: RAND Corporation, R-4150-USDP, 1992.

McCormick, G. H., and G. Gown, "Security and Coordination in Clandestine Organization," *Mathematical and Computer Modelling*, No. 31, 2000.

McDermott, Jeremy, "War Resumes After Collapse of Colombian Peace Process," *Jane's Intelligence Review*, April 2002.

McDonald, Henry, "IRA Manuals Discovered in Colombia," *Guardian Unlimited*, December 16, 2001, www.observer.co.uk/nireland/story/0,11008,619668,00.html (accessed September 2003).

McGeary, Johanna, "Hamas: Popular, Extreme, and an Alternative to Arafat," *Time*, Vol. 158, No. 26, 2001.

Miller, T. Christian, "The Alleged Brains Behind Bin Laden," *Los Angeles Times*, October 2, 2001, www.latimes.com/news/nation world/world/la-100201egyptian.story (accessed September 2003).

Mishal, Shaul, *Speaking Stones*, Syracuse, N.Y.: Syracuse University Press, 1994.

Mishal, Shaul, and Avraham Sela, *The Palestinian Hamas*, New York: Columbia University Press, 2000.

"Los Misiles de las Farc," *Semana*, September 6, 1999.

Molnar, Andrew R., *Undergrounds in Insurgent, Revolutionary, and Resistance Warfare*, Washington, D.C.: American University, 1963.

_____, *Human Factors Considerations of Undergrounds in Insurgencies*, Hawaii: Special Operations Research Office of the American University, University of the Pacific Press, 1972 (reprinted 2001).

"More Christians Killed in Pakistan," *CBSNews.com*, September 26, 2002, www.cbsnews.com/stories/2002/09/18/world/main522447.shtml (accessed September 2003).

Naeem, Jawad, "Pakistan Joins War Against Al-Qaeda in Its Tribal Areas," *Christian Science Monitor*, June 28, 2002.

Nelan, Bruce W., "What's Peace Got to Do with It?" *Time*, August 9, 1993.

"The Old West Comes to Israel," *Asia Times*, November 16, 2002.

O'Neill, Bard, *Insurgency and Terrorism: Inside Modern Revolutionary Warfare*, Washington, D.C.: Brassey's, 1990.

"Osama Bin Laden v. the U.S.: Edicts and Statements," *Frontline* [PBS Online], 2001, www.pbs.org/wgbh/pages/frontline/shows/binladen/who/edicts.html (accessed September 2003).

"El Otro Plan Colombia," *Cambio*, March 20, 2000.

Palmer, David Scott, ed., *The Shining Path of Peru*, 2nd edition, New York: St. Martin's Press, 1994.

_____, "The Revolutionary Terrorism of Peru's Shining Path," i n Crenshaw (1995).

Parachini, John, "Comparing Motives and Outcomes of Mass Casualty Terrorism Involving Conventional and Unconventional Weapons," *Studies in Conflict and Terrorism*, No. 24, 2001.

"Paramilitaries: The Real IRA/32-County Sovereignty Committee," British Broadcasting Corporation, at www.bbc.co.uk/history/war/troubles/factfiles/rira.shtml (accessed September 2003)

"La Paz Sobre la Mesa," *Cambio*, May 11, 1998.

Pincus, Walter, "Spain Says Al-Qaeda Suspect Videotaped Towers, Other Landmarks," *Washington Post*, July 17, 2002.

"Los Planes de las Farc," *Semana*, August 7, 2000.

"Profile: Abu Sayyaf," *Online NewsHour*, January 2002, www.pbs.org/newshour/terrorism/international/abu_sayyaf.html (accessed September 2003).

Rabasa, Angel, and Peter Chalk, *The Colombian Labyrinth: The Synergy of Drugs and Insurgency and Its Implications for Regional Stability*, Santa Monica, Calif.: RAND Corporation, MR-1339-AF, 2001.

Ramati, Yohanan, "Islamic Fundamentalism Gaining," *Midstream*, Vol. 39, No. 2, 1993.

RAND Terrorism Chronology, available online at http://db.mipt.org.

Ranstorp, Magnus, "Hezbollah's Future?" *Jane's Intelligence Review*, February 1, 1995.

"The Real IRA Split as Warning Is Given," *Guardian Unlimited*, October 22, 2002.

Reich, Walter, *Origins of Terrorism*, Washington, D.C.: Woodrow Wilson Center Press, 1998.

Reid, Robert, "The Philippines' Abu Sayyaf: Bandits or International Terrorists?" Associated Press, April 6, 1995.

Reinfeld, Moshe, and Yossi Melman, "Court Okays Naming Alleged Jewish Spy," *Ha'aretz*, July 12, 2002.

Ricks, Thomas E., and Vernon Loeb, "Afghan War Faltering, Military Leader Says," *Washington Post*, November 8, 2002.

Roberts, Brad, ed., *Hype or Reality? The "New Terrorism" and Mass Casualty Attacks*, Alexandria, Va.: Chemical and Biological Arms Control Institute, 2000.

Saad-Ghorayeb, Amal, *Hizbu'llah: Politics and Religion*, London: Pluto Press, 2002.

"Salafist Group for Call and Combat," FAS Intelligence Resource Program, May 21, 2002, www.fas.org/irp/world/para/salaf.htm (accessed September 2003).

Schmidt, Corinne, "Guzmán Fights on from the Cage," *The Times* [London], September 26, 1992.

Shadmi, Haim, "Suicide Bombers May Have Had Hepatitis," *Ha'aretz*, June 21, 2001.

"El Silencio de las Armas," *Cambio,* August 14, 2000.

Sobelman, Daniel, "Hizbullah Lends Its Services to the Palestinian Intifada," *Jane's Intelligence Review*, November 1, 2001.

"Soldiers Capture Main Camp of Rebel Abu Sayyaf Group," *BBC News* [online], July 19, 1997.

Stern, Jessica, *The Ultimate Terrorists,* Cambridge, Mass.: Harvard University Press, 1999.

Tamayo, Juan, "Colombia's FARC Has a CD, Too," *Miami Herald,* August 13, 2001.

Tan, Andrew, "Armed Muslim Separatist Rebellion in Southeast Asia: Persistence, Prospects, and Implications," *Studies in Conflict and Terrorism*, Vol. 23, February 2000.

"Tapes Shed New Light on Bin Laden's Network," *CNN.com*, August 19, 2002.

Tarazona-Sevillano, Gabriela, "The Organization of the Shining Path," in Palmer (1994).

Tarrow, Sidney, *Power in Movement: Social Movements, Collective Action and Politics*, Cambridge, UK: Cambridge University Press, 1994.

Theimer, Sharon, "Like Terror Network, Bin Laden's Money Trail Reaches Around the Globe," Associated Press, September 19, 2001, www.globalexchange.org/september11/ap091901.html (accessed September 2003).

"Tide of Insurgency in South East Asia," *Jane's Terrorism and Security Monitor*, May 1, 2000.

Tiglao, Rigoberto, "Terror International: Manila Claims Foreign Groups Support Extremists," *Far Eastern Economic Review*, May 4, 1995.

_____, "To Fight or Not to Fight," *Far Eastern Economic Review,* March 9, 1999.

"Traces of Terror: Sept. 11 Attacks Planned in '99, Germans Learn," *New York Times*, August 30, 2002.

"Ulster Peace: How Fragile?" *New York Times*, February 3, 1995.

U.S. Department of Justice, *Al Qaeda Training Manual*, excerpts found at www.usdoj.gov/ag/trainingmanual.htm (updated October 2002; accessed September 2003).

_____, "Six Additional Members of the Abu Sayyaf Group Indicted in Connection with Hostage-Taking and Murder of Americans and Others in the Philippines," press release, December 10, 2002.

U.S. Department of State, *Patterns of Global Terrorism*, 1999.

_____, *Patterns of Global Terrorism*, April 2001.

_____, Bureau of Democracy, Human Rights, and Labor, "Country Reports Human Rights Practices: 2001," March 4, 2002, at www.state.gov/g/drl/rls/hrrpt/2001/wha/8326.htm (accessed August 2003).

U.S. Information Agency, "U.S. Court Document Links Bombing Suspect to Bin Ladin Organization," press release, August 28, 1998, http://usinfo.state.gov/topical/pol/terror/98090102.htm (accessed September 2003).

"U.S. Military Searching Afghan Mountains for Surviving Militants," *Washington Post*, January 29, 2003.

Van Biema, David, "Why the Bombers Keep Coming," *Time*, Vol. 158, No. 26, December 17, 2001.

"El Voto de Tirofijo," *Semana*, June 29, 1998.

Watson, Russell, and Brook Larmer, "It's Your Turn to Lose," *Newsweek*, September 28, 1992.

"Weak Link in the Anti-Terror Chain," *Far Eastern Economic Review*, October 24, 2002.

Wege, Carl Anthony, "Hizbollah Organization," *Studies in Conflict and Terrorism*, Vol. 17, 1994.

"What If He Isn't Guilty?" *Far Eastern Economic Review*, November 7, 2002.

"Who Are the Abu Sayyaf?" *BBC News* [online], June 1, 2001.

Wilson, Scott, "Interview with Carlos Castano, Head of the United Self-Defense Forces of Colombia," *Washington Post*, March 12, 2001.

Wright, Lawrence, "The Man Behind Bin Laden," *The New Yorker*, September 16, 2002.

Zaynah, Abduh, "Report on Ayman Al-Zawahiri's Life, Connection with Bin Laden," *Al-Sharq al-Awsat*, September 22, 2001.